From Starting Small to Winning Big

From Starting Small to Winning Big

The Definitive Digital Marketing Guide for Startup Entrepreneurs

Shishir Mishra

BEP BUSINESS EXPERT PRESS

First published in 2020 by
Business Expert Press, LLC
222 East 46th Street, New York, NY 10017
www.businessexpertpress.com

ISBN-13: 978-1-95152-782-2 (paperback)
ISBN-13: 978-1-95152-787-7 (e-book)

Business Expert Press Entrepreneurship and Small Business Management Collection

Collection ISSN: 1946-5653 (print)
Collection ISSN: 1946-5661 (electronic)

First edition: 2020

10 9 8 7 6 5 4 3 2 1

Printed in the United States of America.

Dedicated to the two most important women in my life,
my mother and my wife

Abstract

Digital Marketing Guide for Startup Entrepreneurs is a practical, step-by-step guide that will help budding entrepreneurs in setting up and executing their digital marketing strategy from scratch to achieve the goals they have set for their startups.

The topics covered in this book such as Search Engine Optimization, Content Marketing, Social Media Marketing, Search Engine Marketing, and Online Reputation Management, are essential for entrepreneurs to learn and master for the success of their startup.

This book guides entrepreneurs in establishing a digital presence of their startups to jet fuel their business growth. The book comes from real-life examples and insights gained from executing digital marketing strategies for startups and small businesses.

This book is perfect for startup entrepreneurs, founders, marketers, and small-business owners who are unaware of digital marketing concepts and how to use digital marketing for their advantage. This book will give them practical tips on applying digital marketing to increase their brand awareness and sales.

Most of the books available in the market on Digital Marketing have theoretical concepts and a lot of pages. A startup entrepreneur with a time crunch finds it difficult to read these books and implement the concepts. *Digital Marketing Guide for Startup Entrepreneurs* is concise and can be completed in one or two sittings. This book will serve as a reference guide for the startup entrepreneurs to which they can always come back to while setting up and executing their digital marketing strategy.

Keywords

digital marketing for startups; internet marketing; digital marketing strategy; search engine optimization; Google Ads; social media marketing; content marketing; Facebook Ads; Google Ads Twitter Ads; SEO; Google Adwords; Google Analytics; ORM; website design fundamentals; digital marketing basics; online reputation management; on-page optimization; on-page SEO; backlinking techniques; off-page SEO; technical SEO; Linkedin Ads

Contents

Introduction

Overview

The people who look at the world differently have always inspired me. These people make decisions and take actions to turn their ideas into reality. For them, every failure is an opportunity to learn, and every victory a promise that they can achieve more. Their age, experience, education, resources, situation, or anything outside their sphere of control does not restrict them. Their discipline, persistence, and resilience are the fuel that keeps them going in the face of difficulties.

No prize for guessing. I am talking about startup entrepreneurs. Throughout my career, I have closely worked with startup entrepreneurs who are self-driven and focused on achieving the goals they set for themselves.

As a startup entrepreneur, you would have an idea for your business, a product line, or a catalog of services you would offer. Apart from what your startup offers, how you will reach out to your potential customers decides the success of your startup?

This book is all about how you can reach out to your target audience and convert them into your loyal customers using digital platforms over the Internet.

Purpose

The purpose of this book is to introduce digital marketing concepts to startup entrepreneurs and provide them with easy action steps that they can take to achieve their business goals.

Whether you are a student planning to start your venture or a well-established entrepreneur, the working knowledge of digital marketing is essential for your success.

A business owner with sound knowledge of digital marketing will always have an edge over its competitors. Moreover, your startup idea would be close to your heart, and you should be actively involved in how you want to market that idea to the right audience.

Even if you plan to hire a digital agency or establish a digital marketing team for your startup, you should have a working knowledge of digital marketing to be a part of strategy formation and to measure the ROI of your digital marketing efforts.

As a consultant, I have helped many startups in creating and executing their digital marketing strategies to achieve their goals. This book contains the real world knowledge that I have gained through my experience as a digital marketer in an easy to understand way. I have used a lot of examples throughout the book to which an entrepreneur can relate.

You can not only use this book at the beginning of your digital marketing journey, but it can also be used to make improvements in your existing digital marketing strategy.

This book contains the necessary basics you need to know to build a strong foundation for your digital marketing strategy. The digital marketing industry is evolving as new technologies, tools, and methodologies are introduced, but one thing that doesn't change is the foundation on which it is built. You can always keep this book handy for reference whenever you are looking for ideas, answers, or solutions while creating and implementing your digital marketing strategy.

Limitations

This book gives you in-depth knowledge of digital marketing concepts, strategies, and various tools that you will be using for your startup, although it doesn't cover some advanced concepts and procedures that are used by seasoned digital marketing professionals. The reason to not include them in this book is that these advanced concepts are only useful once you have mastered the digital marketing concepts discussed in this book.

However, this book exhaustively covers the information you will need to execute your digital marketing as a beginner and will be your reference point as you move to an intermediary stage as a digital marketer with experience.

This book will help you to take your startup from an idea to a well-established brand online and help you open up different streams of revenue for your business.

Disclaimer

The various tools mentioned in this book such as Google Analytics, Google Ads, Facebook, LinkedIn, and Twitter advertising platforms, etc, keeps updating their user interfaces. The user interface screenshots used in this book are depicting the user interfaces of the tools at the time the screenshots were taken. The current user face of these tools may slightly differ from the user interface screenshots in the book. However, the basics of using these tools remain the same as described in the book.

CHAPTER 1

Fundamentals of Digital Marketing

Digital marketing is a means to achieve your business goals using the Internet and digital platforms such as search engines, social media, business listing websites, e-commerce portals, and so on.

Benefits of Digital Marketing

Let's rewind the clock backward: remember the time when you were a teenager, and you saw a new TV commercial of denim jeans. You got a strong urge to go to the mall and buy those denim jeans. You got a sense of accomplishment as you purchased the latest fashion denim jeans before any of your friends in your neighborhood.

Let's look at it from the advertising agency's standpoint that created the TV commercial. Their goal was to successfully launch a new clothing line in the market and increase sales of the denim jeans through their advertisement. The agency created an exciting commercial for the television and ran the ad during a famous MTV show as the target audience for their clothing line was teenagers.

The manufacturer of the clothing line invested heavily in the advertisement. There was a substantial increase in sales of denim jeans. But the ad agency will never get to know how many teenagers watched their ads and how many of them did purchase the jeans. This is a traditional form of marketing in which the marketer was driven by gut feeling or intuition on the performance of their ad campaigns rather than facts or data.

Now let's look at a similar scenario and see how digital marketing can be a game-changer? Melissa is a fashion designer; she is very famous among her friends for her trendy t-shirt designs. She was so far designing the t-shirts for her friends and her acquaintances. Melissa was able to sell her designer t-shirts through strong word-of-mouth publicity. Motivated by her initial success, she plans to promote her designs to a broader audience and sell her t-shirts online. She takes the help of her college friend Nick who is studying digital marketing.

Nick creates a four-page website and a Facebook ad for Melissa's t-shirt brand. He sets the target audience for the Facebook ad as the students in her college. So everyone in his college who is on Facebook can see the ad.

Nick also sets up a tracking code on Melissa's website to see how many people purchased the t-shirt after viewing the Facebook ad. Melissa was able to sell 30 t-shirts in a week, and she invested roughly the cost of two t-shirts in the Facebook ad and her website. She shared 20 percent of the profits with Nick.

Melissa, with the help of Nick, was able to not only sell her designer t-shirts online, but she was also able to identify the t-shirts designs that were higher in demand.

The crux of the story is that digital marketing levels the playing field. Before digital media took shape, only deep-pocketed businesses who were able to buy media time on television and radio could promote their offerings. Digital marketing offers a more affordable way to reach a broad target audience. It gives marketers data-driven insights on their target audience and their buying behavior.

The most important question that comes to your mind will be how digital marketing does that?

Well! This book is all about how to achieve your business goals with the help of digital marketing. You need to first know the advantages of digital marketing over traditional marketing to get started.

Benefits: Digital Marketing Over Traditional Marketing

1. Digital Marketing is cheaper than traditional marketing
   Traditional marketing is done through the following media:
   - Print
   - Television
   - Radio

- Flyers and billboards
- Events

The conventional forms of advertising, like running a TV commercial, print ads, radio ads, and so on, require huge investments, whereas digital marketing is inexpensive, and it has the capacity to reach a broad target audience.

There are two types of digital marketing:

- Organic
- Inorganic

Organic marketing is a natural, authentic, value-based approach to drive traffic to your website and develop brand voice over some time. This is a form of inbound marketing approach in which you educate your target audience through blogs and convert blog readers as potential customers. Organic marketing that takes leverage of search engine optimization is virtually free.

Inorganic marketing, in other words, is paid marketing that allows a business to target, engage, and convert their audiences directly and quickly. Inorganic marketing is a push strategy in which you push your content to the target audience in the form of ads. Inorganic marketing, which is done with the help of Facebook ads, Twitter ads, LinkedIn ads, and so on, gives more control over your budget and ad spend.

2. Digital marketing helps you reach a larger audience

There are over 4 billion users of the Internet, which is more than half of the world's population. Every single day, there are more than 3.5 billion searches on Google. The number of Internet users is ever increasing, and with the advent of smartphones, the number of mobile Internet users also keeps growing. Imagine the visibility your business could get over the Internet.

With the help of the Internet, you can reach out to your potential customers, even on the other side of the globe. The television and radio commercials are limited to a geographical region, whereas people can view your Internet ads anywhere across the world.

3. Digital marketing helps you precisely target the right audience

The level of precision you get while targeting your audience through digital marketing could not be achieved by traditional marketing. Using digital marketing platforms such as Facebook, you can target your ideal audience based on their interests, demographics, location, preferences, and lot more.

While running a re-marketing campaign, you can choose to reach out to only those audiences who have engaged with your previous campaign. You can also choose to create a "lookalike audience" that includes people whose online behavior is similar to your current customers. With a traditional form of marketing, you will have to target at a broader level based on demographics, location, and so on. You will be more driven by assumptions and perceptions rather than actual data.

4. Digital marketing helps you accurately measure the effectiveness of your efforts

This is the reason why marketers love digital marketing. Various free and paid tools allow you to measure the effectiveness of your marketing efforts accurately.

Let's take an example; a travel startup sets up a blogging site. The primary purpose of their blogs is to get the blog readers to sign-up a form to talk to a travel advisor.

The travel startup also would set up a Google Analytics account to monitor their website's blog performance. With the help of Google Analytics, they were able to know how many visitors are reading their blogs, which blogs are most popular, and which blogs are getting more sign-ups.

They even got to know which kind of blogs they should publish on their website to get more form sign-ups. You can also gain a similar level of insights from your website. This is covered later in the chapter on Google Analytics in this book.

This level of insights is unimaginable and impossible to achieve through traditional marketing. A small restaurant using flyers to promote their home delivery service will never come to know how many people received their flyers. How many people ordered from their restaurant reading their pamphlets? This information is not available in the traditional form of marketing.

In digital marketing, you can measure the performance of your paid ads. You can measure the return on investment of your paid campaigns. You can gain actionable insights on how to tweak your ads to get a higher return on investment.

5. Digital marketing helps you build a powerful brand

Digital marketing helps you establish a strong brand presence online. You can gain a higher brand recall among your target audience with your digital marketing efforts. You can target the same people on different platforms to achieve higher visibility and create brand awareness.

Let's take an example; you own a store that sells gift cards online in Santa Barbara. You have created a website and optimized it for search engines. This means that when anyone searches by typing in "buy gift cards in Santa Barbara" or "buy birthday cards in Santa Barbara," on Google, your website shows up in the first three search results of Google.

You also run Facebook Ads for people located in Santa Barbara who are interested in gift cards or who have visited your website once. You also run a campaign on your Instagram account to promote your gift cards in Santa Barbara.

This way, your targeted audience will be able to see your brand through search engines, Facebook, and Instagram. Your brand will have higher brand recognition and recall value among people in Santa Barbara who are interested in gift cards.

These are the high-level benefits of digital marketing. There are certain benefits that you will experience yourself when you start implementing your digital marketing strategy.

Digital marketing provides many benefits over traditional marketing, but it doesn't mean you should altogether ditch traditional marketing. Businesses are now providing their customers with an omnichannel experience, which means they are integrating different channels to offer a more seamless experience.

The omnichannel approach lets you integrate your online as well as offline marketing efforts to deliver a message about your brand, which is consistent across all channels whether it is on the digital channels such as your website, Facebook page, Instagram page, and so on, or the message on your flyers, brochures, print ads, and so on.

Disney is one good example of omnichannel integration. They provide you a mobile app that not only allows you to book tickets online but once you are in the park, you can use their app to locate different characters on their live map. You can also get your photographs clicked at their stores and get your pictures on Disney's mobile app.

Facets of Digital Marketing

Digital marketing is a combination of all your marketing efforts through digital channels with the help of the Internet. There are some crucial elements that should be a part of your digital marketing.

Whether you are in a business-to-customer (B2C) domain or you are in the business-to-business (B2B) field, you should include these elements in your digital marketing strategy.

Let's take a look at the essential facets of digital marketing.

Website

You might have a favorite restaurant that you would want to visit more often than any other restaurant. Maybe it's because of the food, the ambiance, the service you get, or perhaps it is because of the live music.

Similarly, you would like to visit a website if it's visually appealing and the content informative and useful to you. You feel good while browsing the site.

For your business, the most critical digital asset is your website. Your website represents your business online.

Your website should be one of the key differentiators for your business. A startup with a visually appealing and engaging website can outperform a big brand online that has a poorly designed website.

The goal of a website may be different for different businesses, but for a website to succeed, the great visitor experience is a must.

In the next chapter of this book, you will learn how to create a website that helps to grow your business. If you already have an existing website, you can learn how to improve your website for creating more opportunities for your business.

Content Marketing Strategy

The content marketing strategy is all-inclusive of creating content and distributing it to the targeted audience. The purpose of creating a content marketing strategy may be to generate leads, build brand awareness, or to fulfill any other marketing goals.

Your content marketing strategy will include answers to the following questions:

- What is the end goal you want to achieve with your content?
- For whom you will create the content?
- Which kind of content will be helpful for your target audience?
- What makes your content unique?
- How your target audience will find your content online?
- How often will you create content?
- How will you monitor the performance of your content?

If you already have content that you have created in the past, you need to do a content audit. You need to find answers to the questions listed above. If you don't see a satisfactory response, you need to make changes to your content marketing strategy.

The content you create for your business online should not only be useful for your target audience, but it should be easily discoverable by the search engines.

In my experience, I have come across many websites that are just written for search engines (search engine optimized content). The content will have all the keywords that the users are typing in the search engine to find the information. When you only focus on search engines, your content lacks information quotient. Such material is not useful for your target audience.

There can also be an instance in which the content is written with a high level of research, and it offers excellent insights, but it is not optimized for search engines, which means it is not easily discoverable.

You need to strike a balance between how the users will find the content (search engine friendly content) and how much value the material will create for the users (user-friendly content).

There are different formats of content that can be posted online, such as:

- Blog posts
- E-books
- Case studies
- Templates
- Infographics
- Videos
- Podcasts
- Social media posts

You will have to find the type of content that is most suitable for your audience, depending on your industry.

Search Engine Optimization

Nowadays, we all are dependent on search engines to find information easily and quickly. Whether you are searching for a restaurant, planning your next trip, or searching for some information, you turn to Google. There are several search engines such as Google, Bing, Yahoo, Duck-DuckGo, that help you find any content online.

Let's understand this with an example. You are searching for a restaurant that serves Mexican food in your vicinity. You open Google in your browser and type in the keyword "Mexican food near me." Google will ask you to allow it to "Know your location" if you have not already shared your location with Google.

Now the Google search engine will bring back the search results from the websites that have optimized any of their pages with the keyword "Mexican food" in your location. Even if there is a good restaurant in your vicinity that serves excellent Mexican food, but they have not optimized their website for the keyword "Mexican food," you will not see their website in your Google search results. So you will only get the sites that are search engine optimized in your search results.

In simpler terms, search engine optimization is the process of making your website discoverable on search engines by a maximum number of people. You need to ensure your site appears at the top of the search results on your selected keywords.

Social Media Marketing

Social media marketing is the form of digital marketing in which content is created and distributed via social media networks such as Facebook, Twitter, LinkedIn, and so on. It has become the most effective form of marketing online, whether you are running paid campaigns or doing it organically (without paid campaigns). You may have come across many viral videos. Some of the viral videos are created by brands to get higher visibility and greater reach in a short period.

Social media platforms allow you to target audiences with unprecedented levels of accuracy. Facebook allows you to target users based on their location, their interests, their level of engagement with ad campaigns, and the kind of user information that is a potential goldmine for a marketer.

Any business, whether big or small, cannot afford to lose the opportunity created by social networks in creating highly personalized campaigns with a higher level of engagement.

Search Engine Marketing

Search engine marketing (SEM), more popularly known as PPC (pay per click) advertising is used to run paid ads in the search engine results. These ads are run using search engine platforms such as Google Ads, Bing Ads, and Yahoo: Search Ads. These platforms allow users to bid for keywords used in the search query to show paid ads in search results.

Let's take an example, type in "Buy sports shoes" in your Google search engine. In the search results, the first two to three results with ads denoted in front of the website URL are the results on which paid ads are running through Google Ads.

Google's paid search ads help your brand to get on the first page of Google search results, especially the search intent of the user is to make a purchase. In the search results, the first search result page is the place where all the action happens. The top three search results on the first page of search results get the maximum traffic (visitors) on their website.

There is a famous joke among digital marketers that if you want to hide a dead body, you can hide it on the third page of Google search results. Nobody goes to the third page of the Google search results. If you want to get visitors and leads (potential customers), you should aim to make your brand visible in the first two pages of search results.

Analytics

Digital marketing analytics gives a marketer the power to understand the effectiveness of their marketing strategy. You can easily measure the contribution and ROI of your marketing initiatives.

You can analyze the behavior of the visitors on your website or the people who have engaged with your campaigns (social media, e-mail marketing, blogging, etc.) to get actionable insights that can help you grow your business.

Google Analytics is a free to use tool that you can use for your website to analyze your marketing efforts more effectively. You can know which of your online channels is performing the best, whether it's your website blogs, your social media channels, your paid campaigns, or the referral traffic (visitors from other websites linking to your site).

Digital analytics should be an integral part of your digital marketing. It helps you to improve your strategy to get better results. With digital analytics, you don't have to wait for a long time to know whether you are doing the right things or not.

All these facets or critical elements of digital marketing are covered in this book in the coming chapters. You will learn the basics of these concepts as well as learn the implementation of each of these aspects of digital marketing.

Digital Marketing Strategy

In simpler terms, the digital marketing strategy is the series of actions you take to achieve your business goals with the help of online marketing channels. The channels include paid, earned, and owned media channels that are used to support a common goal.

Lets first understand what are owned, earned, and paid media.

Owned Media

The owned media is when you leverage a channel that you create and control. This could be your website, your Facebook page, your YouTube channel, or any other social media account that you own. You don't have to pay for the usage of this media.

Earned Media

Earned media is when your customers, press, or anyone shares your content or speak about your brand online. These mentions about your brand given voluntarily are your earned media.

Paid Media

Paid media is when you pay for running advertisements or sponsorship on third-party sites.

You will be leveraging owned, earned, and paid media to implement your digital marketing strategy.

Steps to Formulate Your Digital Marketing Strategy

1. Set the goals you want to achieve with your digital marketing strategy

   The first step would be to precisely know what you want to accomplish with your digital marketing strategy.

   Let's take an example:

You have a travel startup, and your business goal is to book more trips for the customers. For this, you have created a website. Initially, you will have lower brand awareness for your startup. One of your goals will be to increase your business's brand awareness.

High-level goal: To increase brand awareness

Now to increase your brand awareness, you need several visitors on your website. So a more tangible and measurable goal would be outlining exactly how many visitors you want on your website monthly. So a better digital marketing goal for your business would be such as below:

Goal: To get 10,000 monthly visitors on your website in the next three months.

You should have an exact number of visitors and the exact date by when you will achieve your goal.

You should list down at least three goals to achieve through your digital marketing strategy.

Here are a few examples of digital marketing goals:

- Increase sales by 10 percent from the website by December 2020.
- Increase the number of your Twitter followers by 10 percent by December 2020.
- Double the number of your blog subscribers by December 2010.

2. Create Buyer Personas

This is the most critical step that can make or break your digital marketing strategy. At times a business starts off implementing their digital marketing strategy without even exactly knowing the target audience of their campaigns.

The buyer persona comprises a profile of your target audience that includes their background, motivations, and their challenges along with how your product or service can help in overcoming those challenges.

Let's take an example of a buyer persona for a mobile app for social work.

- *Name of the persona*: Chris
- *Age*: 29
- *Background*: Chris is a young and energetic individual who likes to contribute to social causes.
- *Goals*
    - Want to make a positive difference in his community
    - Looking to connect with like-minded individuals
- *Challenges*
    - Doesn't know how to connect with fellow change-makers
- *How we can help*
    - Provide a platform to create a group who are interested in specific social cause
    - Connect with other people based on common interest
    - Organize meet events to contribute toward a social cause

The buyer persona should give you accurate information as you can get on your target audience. You can always improve your buyer personas based on the insights you gain through tools such as Google Analytics.

3. Plan your digital sales funnel

Now you have your online goals with you, and you know your target audience, the next step would be to plan your digital sales funnel as per the AIDA model. The AIDA model stands for Attention, Interest, Desire, and Action.

- The buying behavior of customers at different stages of interaction with your brand will be different.
    - Attention: The first step is to attract the attention of your potential customers to your brand.
    - Interest: As the customers are aware of your brand, the next step will be to increase their interest level in your brand.
    - Desire: The next step will be to develop a desire to purchase in interested people.
    - Action: The last step of the sales funnel is the action that the customer takes, such as making the purchase.

Let's take an example of how to apply the AIDA model of digital marketing. Eric and his friend Matt created an easy-to-use Project

Management Software for small businesses. Now they want to market their software online.

As per the AIDA model, the first thing they need to do is to get attention toward their brand. Eric created a website and launched a Facebook Ads campaign to target project managers.

The main aim of Facebook Ads was to get visitors on their website. These paid ads help them get attention to their project management software. Now to draw the interest of the project managers, Matt writes search engine optimized blogs that are highly informative and useful for project managers. The project managers read the blogs and subscribe to their blog newsletter by giving their e-mail ids. Now Eric and Matt have an e-mail list of subscribers.

To develop a desire to purchase the software in the project managers, Eric and Matt, start an e-mail campaign that is sent to their blog subscribers. These e-mails not only include the latest blogs published on their website but also include information on the benefits of their project management software.

In the last phase of their digital marketing funnel, they want their website visitors, blog subscribers, e-mail recipients, and so on to take the action of booking a demo with them wherein Eric and Matt can showcase the benefits of using their products. Finally, this will lead to a purchase.

This is an example of how you plan for your digital sales funnel by creating content for all the stages of the AIDA model.

4. Plan for the digital marketing channels you will use

Now you can narrow down the channels you will use to target your buyer personas. Let's say you have a startup that sells home decors. For your business, social networks such as Pinterest and Instagram are ideal for showcasing your items visually.

For planning the digital channels, you need to know which channels your target audience prefers.

To plan for your channels, you can use the same channels used by your competitors. Thorough research of your competitors is essential as you can also look at their strengths and weaknesses while formulating your digital marketing strategy.

You can always include new channels as the trend changes. In this book, you will learn about different channels. As you know more about different channels, you can decide whether a particular channel is suitable for your business or not.

For example, for the B2B industry, LinkedIn is a more suitable channel than Instagram or Facebook.

5. Plan for analyzing the performance

This is the step where you will list down all the tools you will use for monitoring your digital marketing efforts. When it comes to paid ads, every tool that you will be using, such as Google Ads, Facebook, Twitter, or LinkedIn provides you with dashboards to monitor your performance. To monitor the performance of your SEO, you can take leverage of some free and paid tools.

Google Analytics would be the best free tool at the initial stage of your digital marketing strategy. You will get to know how to gain insights into your data and how to feed the ideas into your digital marketing strategy. There some other marketing tools such as HubSpot, Ahref, SEMrush, and so on that will help you gain insights.

You have now learned the basics of digital marketing, its advantages, the different facets, and how to craft your digital marketing strategy. In the chapters that follow, you will get to learn how to implement a successful digital marketing strategy.

Points to Remember

1. Digital marketing is a means to achieve your business goals with the help of Internet and digital platforms.
2. Digital marketing is inexpensive and it allows small businesses to reach a broad target audience.
3. You can target your ideal audiences based on their interests, demographics, location, preferences, and lot more.
4. You can gain a higher brand recall with your digital marketing efforts.
5. For a website to succeed, it must offer a great visitor experience.
6. The content marketing strategy includes creating content and distributing it to the targeted audience.
7. Search engine optimization (SEO) is done to make your website findable on search engines by a maximum number of people.

8. Social media platforms allow you to target audiences with unprece-dented levels of accuracy.

9. Digital marketing analytics gives a marketer the power to understand the effectiveness of their marketing strategy.

10. Digital marketing strategies include all the actions you need to take to achieve your business goals with the help of online marketing channels.

11. You should list down at least three goals you want to accomplish through your digital marketing strategy.

12. You need to plan your digital sales funnel as per the AIDA model. The AIDA model stands for Attention, Interest, Desire, and Action.

13. The buyer persona is creating a profile of your target audience in a way to include their background, motivations, challenges, and how your product or service can help in overcoming those challenges.

14. Identify the channels you will use to target the audience.

15. Monitoring your digital marketing efforts will help you improve your overall strategy and execution.

Assignment

1. List down three goals you wish to achieve through your digital mar-keting efforts.

2. Create three buyer personas of your target audience.

3. Research at least three close competitors of your business. Visit their website, their social channels such as their Facebook, Twitter, and so on. List down what you liked and disliked about their digital channels.

CHAPTER 2

Website Design: Tips and Tricks

A website represents a business online. It allows your business to be available anytime and accessible from anywhere in the world. The purpose of your website is to build your brand image and increase the sales of your business offerings.

A website that is designed in tune with your digital marketing goals will be successful for your business.

For example, if you want to increase the sales of your products, then your whole website should support this purpose. It should be easy to find information on the site, which will help the visitor in making the purchase decision. The process of making the purchase should be effortless.

Website Planning

Any website is created for some purpose. The success of a website is measured in terms of how effectively the website serves the purpose.

1. *Determine the purpose of the website*

You must determine the purpose of your website: what you intend to achieve through your website. When you know precisely the goal of your website, you can plan for the elements on your website that will help you achieve your goals.

These are some of the goals you can set for your website:

- Get more traffic and leads (potential customers) from your website
- Increase brand awareness
- Improve user satisfaction
- Increase direct sales from website
- Establish thought leadership

2. Analyze your competitors

You should always start with competitor research. You must be aware of who your competitors are and the market leader in your industry.

If you want to know about your competitors online, just use the keywords that someone would use to find your business in the search engines. You will find the pages of your competitors in the search results.

Do preliminary research on the website of your competitors. You can analyze the strength and weaknesses of the website of your competitors. The market research of your competitor's website will help you understand the common ingredients that the websites in your industry have. You can list down the sites that you find inspiring in terms of design and content.

The importance of competitor analysis is that you will get a lot of ideas on what kind of information and design you need for your website. You can list down all the things that you liked on at least three of your competitor's sites and all the things you disliked.

With competitor research, you will ensure that you don't make a grave mistake while planning for your website.

For example, if you are in a business-to-business domain, and you have designed your website taking inspiration from a business-to-customer site, then your website is doomed to fail.

An e-commerce site is designed in a particular way, while a corporate website is created in some other way. You should innovate with your website design but stick to the pattern of the sites in your industry.

3. Create information architecture and user flows

The information architecture helps you outline the flow of information—what pages you need to keep on your website and what should be a hierarchy of the pages. If you are not sure which information you want on your website, you can refer to the competitor websites you researched previously.

One useful approach would be to use sticky notes to create a site map of your website (Figure 2.1).

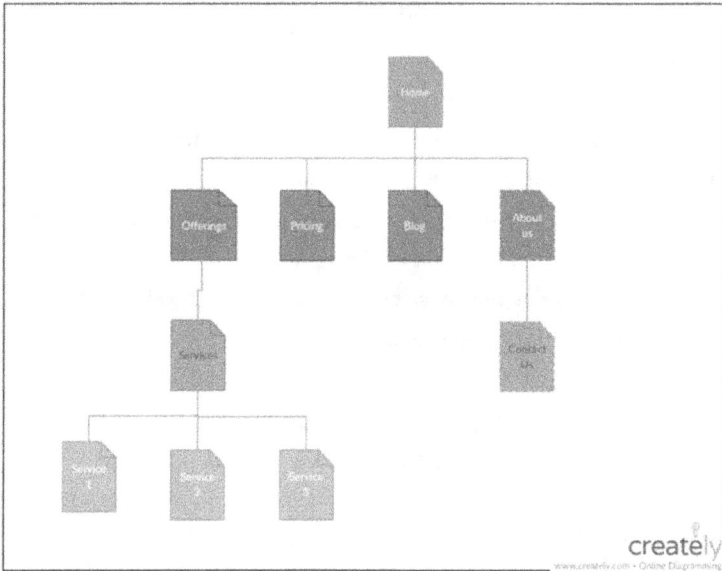

Figure 2.1 Information architecture of a website

You should then describe the user flow of your website. The user flow helps to outline how the user will navigate through different pages of the website. The user flow should be such that it helps the user to take the desired action you want them to take. That could be to make a purchase, sign up a form, start a free trial, and so on.

4. *Outline design elements*

As you create the information architecture and user flow, you need to list down the following design elements.

- Color palette
- Photography or illustration style
- Fonts/ typography
- Use of space
- Navigation style

5. *Create wireframes*

Wireframes help you to define the layout of your web pages—a design that outlines where will be elements such as videos, images, and forms, and so on be placed on a web page and how the navigation of your site will be like. It's like the blueprint of your website.

A wireframe is similar to a blueprint of a house that a construction team needs to know where will be the kitchen, where will be the bedroom, how the pipelines will be connected, and how the electricity lines will run through the house. A miscalculation at the blueprint level could also cost you a lot of time and money.

Wireframes are the most crucial part of your website. You can create a wireframe on a piece of paper. For creating a wireframe, you need to first think of the purpose of your site—if your site offers a service for which you give a free trial. Then the most critical part of your website would be the trial form. You have to make sure how the users will find the trial form on your website and what information will drive website visitors to fill the form.

Website Design Fundamentals

The design of a website helps to establish the credibility of a business. If the website design is not visually appealing, most of the visitors will leave the site before exploring it much.

Here are the website design fundamentals that will help you convert more website visitors into your customers.

Limit the Options

The attention span of website visitors has decreased considerably. The website visitors tend to scroll through the pages, skimming information rather than reading the information thoroughly.

The more the number of choices you present to your website visitors, the lesser is the chance of their taking action.

If your website navigation pane has too many links to browse or you have a long scroll on your home page, you are offering too many choices to your visitors that lower the probability of taking the desired action.

For example, if the landing page of a website offers you to take either of the three actions:

1. To make a purchase
2. To read product reviews
3. To search for more products

These three options will lower the possibility of a visitor from taking any decision at all. The better approach will be to give just a single choice to make a purchase.

If you already have a website for your business, you need to analyze the website starting from the home page. Does your home page give too many options to the visitors that might confuse them?

If you are planning to create a new website or redesign your site, then make sure that all the web pages should drive the visitors to take a single action.

For a Software as a Service (SaaS) website, the call to action in your website could be to take a free trial. For an e-commerce website, the primary call to action would be to add the product in the shopping cart to buy it.

Design for Speed

The website should be designed to ensure the pages load fast. A slow-loading website can make you lose website visitors.

There are many beautifully designed websites with great videos and animations that take more time to load than usual. These websites may have a tremendous visual appeal but most of the visitors don't have time or patience to wait for all the visuals to load.

A good page load speed will also help you in your SEO efforts. You will come to learn about this later.

Here are the tools you can use to check the loading speed of your website:

- Google PageSpeed Insights
- Pingdom

You can search for these tools on Google and analyze the performance of your website.

Use More White Space

The white space is the space between different elements on your website, for example, the space between an image and a heading is white.

You should have more of the white space between not only different elements on your website but also the space between the text. The more breathing space is there for the visuals and the content, the better it would be for your website.

This approach will help you bring more clarity on your website, and it will help to declutter the message. The more white space will increase the readability of the text, and it will also make the images, gifs, or videos to stand out. It will also help you to draw the attention of the users exactly where you want.

The white space is also referred to as negative space. Positive space is that space of the web page that contains all the elements.

Rule of Thirds

There is a famous photography principle that says that you should visually divide an image into thirds (both vertically and horizontally).

The most strategic place of interest is intersections. You should place all the crucial elements on the page on these interactions (Figure 2.2).

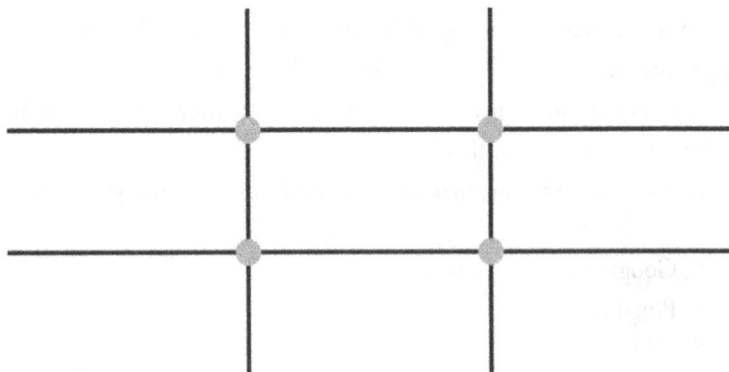

Figure 2.2 Rule of thirds

For example, for a travel website, the button asks you to connect you to the sales team through the button "Talk to us." This button should be placed on one of the intersections.

You can apply this rule to your website and check whether the most essential action buttons are placed on the intersections or not.

F Layout for Placing Elements

Researchers have found that while looking at a web page, people view the content from left to right at the top. As they scan the page downwards, they look from left to right at a lesser section of the web page. This means that the part of the page that will get the least attention is the right most corner of the page (Figure 2.3).

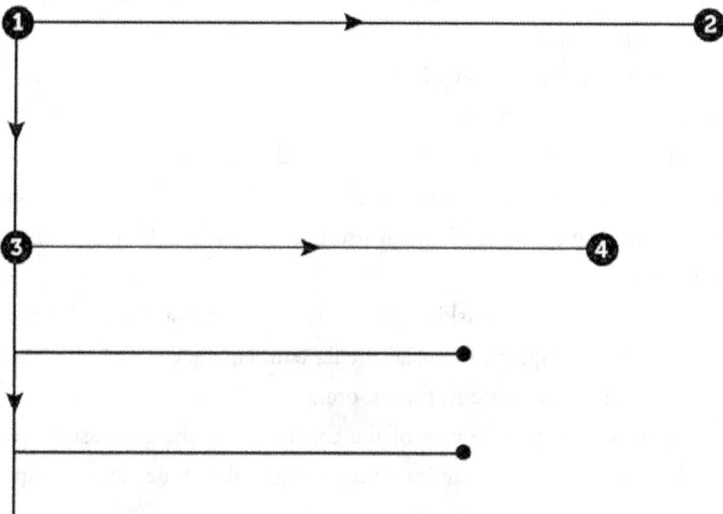

Figure 2.3 F layout for placing elements

This research is based on the heat maps, which show the user's interaction with the webpage. To boost conversion (main action you want your users to take) for your website, you can strategically place different action buttons or credibility building content in an F layout.

This means that the top left corner will have the most critical content. The other useful content should be placed on the left-hand side as we move down toward the bottom of the page.

Use Colors to Build Brand Recognition

When it comes to choosing colors for their website, people tend to go all out and make their website as colorful as possible. At times, the graphic designer tends to go overboard with colors to showcase their creative skills.

A colorful website that doesn't resonate with your brand colors will do more harm than good. The best strategy would be to select the three most essential colors that you will be using throughout all your digital channels.

For example, you have chosen a shade of green, blue, and orange for your website. These three colors should be used predominantly everywhere, whether you are using it for social media banners, blog images, or e-mail marketing campaigns.

Let's say green is your brand color, and your logo is in green. You have kept all the action buttons like "Try Free," "Buy Now," "Get Started" in orange color. You can use blue tones in different elements of the design.

Now where you are asking people to take some action, whether it is your e-mail campaign or social media banner, the color of the action button should be consistent, that is, orange.

You also need to take care of the contrast. Use the contrast to keep your headlines and call-to-action buttons noticeable, for example, using a white background with black text for higher contrast.

I have personally witnessed an example of brand color blunders. It was not precisely displayed on the website but in Google Display Ads.

A digital marketing agency was running a display ad campaign where they were using three different shades of green for the brand, although there was a particular shade of green used for brand color. The blunder was that even after paying heavily for running the ads, the brand recognition and recall value was lower than average.

Keep It Short and Simple (KISS)

The website design trends have evolved to match the lower attention span of the website visitors. The best converting website across the Internet are those who are keeping it simple and having a decluttered interface.

To deliver a great user experience to your website visitors, you should remove anything and everything that is not informative or anyway useful to the visitor.

Apple's website is one of the best examples of the KISS approach. Website copywriters tend to give as much information as possible and use deadwood phrases. These deadwood phrases communicate a lot less in far more words.

Grab Attention in 8 Seconds

The length of the attention span of a website visitor has dwindled to 8 seconds. It means in 8 seconds you have to engage a user to spend more time on your website. If you miss out on those crucial 8 seconds, then your site will struggle with the conversion. To avoid a lower conversion rate, here are the tips you can put into practice:

- Use a concise benefit-driven headline (unique value proposition)
- Use real human images that draw attention to your call to action
- The action buttons should be large and clear
- Use power words such as Prize, Free, Best, Profit, and so on.
- Use video, audio, or any other multimedia format to engage users
- Use hover effects on the action buttons to drive action
- Use exit pop-ups to re-engage visitors who are about to leave your website

Group Elements to Boost Conversion

The human brain likes to group similar objects. You can use this law of grouping items for your benefit in your design by keeping the call-to-action buttons, testimonial boxes, images, and conversion buttons together.

For example, you can use a testimonial box just below your lead conversion form. This will help users to perceive the sign-up form and testimonial as one, and it will help build credibility to drive action.

This also helps to group the other elements on the web page together and separate them from call-to-action form. This way, the call to action gets more emphasis on the overall design.

Use Real Faces to Increase Familiarity

The human faces on your website make the website visitors feel connected with your brand as humans tend to empathize with human faces. When you use human faces on your case studies, articles, landing pages, and any other places, it will help to boost conversion.

The best approach will be to use the faces of real people behind your brand. This will help you to connect on a personal level with your website visitors. If you don't want to use your images, then you can always go for stock images.

High-Quality Images to Boost Conversion

The images you use on your website will significantly impact the engagement and conversion of your website. Using high-quality photos will help you create visual appeal. The pictures of your website should also be optimized for speed.

Using a high-quality image that is over 100 kb will take too much time to load, and it may not load at all on lower Internet speed. The best approach will be to resize your images using an image optimization tool. You can search for a free image-resizing tool on Google.

Mobile-Responsive Design

We are now using smartphones to access the Internet more than desktop and personal computers. It's somewhat easier to browse the web on your mobile phone than to start your computer every time. Therefore your website should be mobile responsive, which means it should look good on mobile screens as well.

A mobile-responsive website will help your business to target mobile users, which you would have overlooked otherwise.

If you already have a website, you can evaluate your site to validate whether these website design fundamentals are met or not. If you are creating a new website for your business, make sure you take into account all these fundamentals in your website design. The more precise you are with the purpose of your website, the more your website will be in line with your business goals.

The website design can be only evaluated in terms of how effectively it serves business goals. The more the design helps the business purpose, the more successful it is.

Website Essentials

Here are the steps to quickly set up a website for your business.

Get a Web Hosting and Register a Domain

You will need to subscribe to a web hosting service to store all the images, content, and website file. As you have a hard disk on your computer to save all your data, you need a web hosting service to save the website files.

You need to register a domain name, which will be the address of your website. This website address will help anyone to reach your site. As your physical address is necessary if some want to visit your house, similarly, you need a domain name to let others find your website online.

While choosing the domain name, make sure it is similar to your brand name. For example, you have a gift store with the name "Gift Corner," then your website should be www.giftcorner.com. This will help in creating brand consistency. At times, the website domain name may not be available as it is already taken. You can tweak the name of your domain a bit.

Some of the popular web hosting service providers are:

- Bluehost
- HostGator
- SiteGround
- GoDaddy

Setting Up Your Website

You will then need a CMS, which is the content management system for your website. You need to install the CMS on your hosting service. The installation of CMS on your web hosting account is an intuitive process.

The most commonly used CMS is WordPress. It helps you design your site easily. There are many themes available that you can customize to suit your business needs. You will get a large number of paid and unpaid plugins to extend the functionality of your website.

Every web hosting service gives you a rather straightforward process to install WordPress. Here are the steps to install WordPress on your Bluehost account. The steps are somewhat similar to any other hosting service.

1. You need to login into your Bluehost hosting account.
2. Go to the control panel section.
3. You can easily locate the WordPress icon.
4. You need to choose the domain where you want to install WordPress.
5. Click the "Install Now" button, and you will be able to access your new WordPress site.

Design Your Website

As you have installed your website, now you can start customizing your site. There many free themes available in WordPress. A theme is a design template that you can use to style your website.

Most of the themes in WordPress are free are to use. You can install a particular theme on your WordPress and customize it.

You need to first login to the admin section of your site https://your-site.com/wp-admin (Here in the place of "your site," use your registered domain nahttps://flyingbakery.com/wp-adminme). For example, if your website is https://flyingbakery.com, then log in.

As you login to the WordPress dashboard, you can click on Appearance on the left sidebar and then click on themes to find all the themes available.

As you Install and Activate a theme, you can start adding content to your website (Figure 2.4).

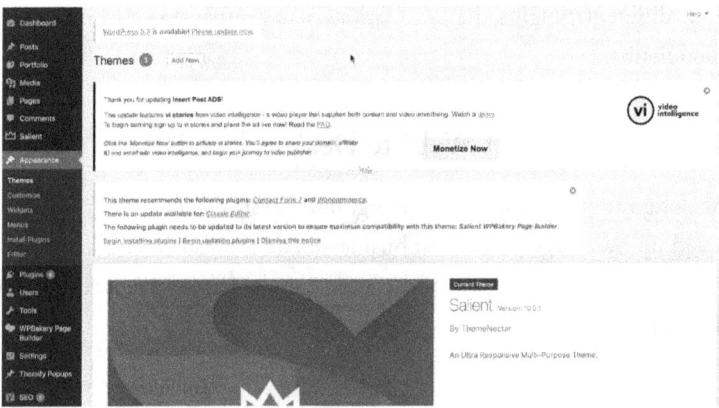

Figure 2.4 Designing your website

Adding Pages

You can add new pages to your site to showcase the services you offer and what your company is all about.

The sidebar in the WordPress Dashboard allows you to add new pages through the "Pages" → "Add New."

You can add images and content of your choice.

Adding Menu

Click on the "Appearance" and then click on "Menus" in the sidebar of the WordPress dashboard. You can add pages to the menu from this section.

Maintaining a Blog Section

To have a blog section on your website, you need "Posts." You can even create a category of different posts.

For example, you have a travel website, and you want to create two different categories, such as "Travel Hacks" and "Destinations." You group your different blogs in these two categories.

To create a new category, you can click on "Posts → Categories."

To learn how to make a powerful WordPress website, you can visit https://wpbeginner.com/. You will find a lot of tutorial videos and blogs that will help you customize your website from scratch. You will learn about different plugins that you can add to your website to extend its functionality.

Latest Website Design Trends

The design trends are always evolving, but a design trend takes time to be picked up by a large number of businesses, and it also takes a lot of time to fade away. Here are some of the latest trends that have gained traction and are here to stay.

Bright Colors

The bright and vibrant colors get more eyeballs than a dull gray background. The bright colors are now being used to get attention. User attention is elusive, especially in the 8 seconds attention span era. If you want to draw attention to your website, you need to stand out. The first way to stand out is through the use of bright colors.

Using Video in the Background

Using video in the background of the home page engages more users than static images. A short video playing in a loop in the background of your home page without audio can get you more engagement. It has always been the design principle to show rather than tell. Video can boost your conversion rate more than any other content format.

Splitting the Screen

One of the design trends that are rather simple yet powerful is splitting the design on the screen into two distinctive yet connected parts. This design technique is rather uncomplicated yet effective. It also works well on the mobile screen as two horizontal panels of the screen can be vertically aligned.

For example, a clothing brand that sells clothes for men and women can use a split-screen technique. In this approach, the left half of the screen can be used to showcase men's fashion, and the right half of the screen can be used to showcase women's fashion.

This technique can be used for any website by splitting the screen to showcase two different yet connected messages.

Bold Typography

As the designers have to design to catch the attention of website visitors, bold typography helps them to give center stage to the most important message. Bold typography makes the content easily readable and dominating other sections of the screen. The bold fonts can be used to showcase the unique value proposition of the brand.

These different tricks and tips will help you to make your website achieve your business goals effectively.

Points to Remember

1. A website represents a business online. It makes a business available anytime and accessible from anywhere in the world.
2. You must be aware of what you plan to achieve through its website.
3. Preliminary research of the website of competitors is an essential part of website planning.
4. The information architecture helps to outline the flow of information.
5. A wireframe outlines where will be elements such as videos, images, and forms, and so on will be placed and the navigation flow of the website.
6. A good website design builds the credibility of a business.
7. The number of action buttons (CTA) should be limited to one or two for website visitors to take the desired action.
8. The website should be designed to facilitate fast loading.
9. More white spaces between different elements on the website help to clearly communicate the message.
10. Follow the law of thirds while placing action buttons on the webpages.
11. The top-left most corner should have the most important content.
12. There should be only three most prominent colors throughout your website. Other colors should get less emphasis and should be used less.

13. Group design elements by keeping the call to action buttons and testimonial boxes together.
14. Using high-quality images creates visual appeal and drives user engagement.
15. A mobile responsive website helps to target mobile users.
16. A web hosting service is required to store all the images, content, and files of your website.
17. The domain name is the address of a website.
18. The most commonly used Content Management System is WordPress.
19. Design trends are always evolving, and a website should be designed in line with the latest trend.

Assignment

1. Visit the website of your top three competitors (one of them should be a market leader) and list down the various main sections of their website.
2. List down all the design elements your competitors have used on their website (videos, images, illustrations, action buttons, search box, etc.)
3. Create a wireframe for your website outlining the design elements, action buttons, forms, and navigation style.
4. Select three colors that represent your brand and which you will be using in the future for all your designs.
5. Create a rough draft of the home page of your website, keeping in mind all the design principles and trends.

CHAPTER 3

Content Marketing Strategy

Content is the backbone of your digital marketing. For everything you will be doing to execute your digital marketing strategy, whether it is writing blogs, running ad campaigns, social media marketing, or e-mail marketing, you would be distributing content.

Digital marketing is rather a means to effectively distribute your content to the right target audience. Even if you are very successful in reaching the right target audience, what you say to them through your content can make or break your brand image.

Whenever you think about creating content, always think in terms of the value of the content for the consumer. At times, businesses get carried away in describing what they are offering rather than talking about how their offering will benefit the end-user. This leads to disengagement of the consumers of that content.

What Is Content Marketing Strategy?

Content marketing is a strategic approach to creating and distributing content to attract and engage a specific target audience and influencing them to take the desired actions that are profitable for the business.

In your content marketing strategy, you will define what kind of content you will be creating, for example, blog posts, infographics, videos, and so on. You will also list down the marketing channels where you will be distributing the content, such as your website, social media channels, listing sites, and so on.

You will specifically outline the target audience for whom you will be creating the content. You can have more than one type of target audience for your business. You need to create different content for different kinds of target audience. You will also be using different channels to deliver content to different varieties of target audience.

Your content marketing strategy defines the goals you want to accomplish for your business. Then the most important aspect of your content strategy would be what is your unique value proposition. In simpler terms, what makes your content stand out from your competitors? Why should your customers be reading or viewing your content rather than the content of your competitors?

In a nutshell, your content marketing strategy will give answers to the following questions:

- What are the goals you wish to achieve for your business?
- Who is your target audience?
- What are the pain points of your customers that you wish to address through your content?
- What will make your content unique?
- What is the type of content you will create?
- Which channels will you use to distribute your content to reach out to the target audience?
- How often will you create content?

To cater to your audience, the kind of content that will create the desired results, you need to have a content marketing strategy.

Why Do You Need to Create a Content Marketing Strategy?

You can start by publishing blogs, start tweeting, publishing posts on Facebook, but why you need a content marketing strategy?

Without your content marketing strategy, it's like hunting in the dark. You will never be able to align your content with your conversion goals if you don't have a content marketing strategy in place. Here is why you need a content marketing strategy.

To Ensure Cohesiveness

You will be circulating your content on different channels and a variety of mediums. You need to ensure that on all different channels and mediums where your content is available should have an underlying connection.

If you are writing about certain topics on your blogs, you should be discussing similar topics in your social media posts. Your e-mail marketing should be connected to the same topics.

For example, a website of a web-based tool for software testing professionals publishes blogs related to software testing. Its social media posts should also discuss topics that are related to software testing. Their e-mails address the concerns of software testing professionals. This way, the overall theme of the content is the same across the channels and targets the same audience.

To Create a Brand Identity

Creating a brand identity will help you stand out from the clutter of the competition. It's not what you say that is most important, but how you say it becomes more important. Certain brands are very casual in their communication. Their website content is also very personalized, and all their communication also reflects a personal tone.

Some brands stand out with a pinch of humor. Your brand identity must resonate with your target audience. If your business caters to the teenage population, then your brand identity should resonate with something that is cool, energetic, and adventurous. While creating your brand identity, you can use your buyer personas to know what would be the brand identity that your potential customers want to be associated with.

To Measure Content Marketing Productivity

With a documented content marketing strategy, you can very well measure how effectively you are executing it. If you are planning to publish two blog posts per week according to your content marketing strategy, failing to do so will let you know whether you need more resources to create the quantity of content you want to publish. It also helps you know whether your documented content marketing strategy is realistic and achievable or not.

To Evolve Content Marketing Strategy

You need to evolve your content marketing strategy to stay competitive and effective. With your documented content marketing strategy, you will be able to know whether you are failing or succeeding with your content marketing strategy.

As you start executing your content strategy, you will get measurable results, which will help you know how you are doing.

You need to tweak your content marketing strategy continuously. For example, if you have planned to publish four blog posts per month and you fall short by 25 percent of the number of visitors you want on your website every month. In this case, you can double your number of blog posts published every month to eight blog posts and analyze whether you reach your traffic goal or not. You can also target keywords that have a higher potential of getting traffic.

Similarly, you will have to make changes in your content marketing strategy to accommodate new goals and conversion points.

How to Create a Content Marketing Strategy?

You need to have documented content marketing strategy, which you can continuously update as you get insights from executing your existing strategy.

The following steps can be followed to create a content marketing strategy:

1. Define the business goals you want to achieve
   Some of the business goals you wish to accomplish through your content marketing strategy can be:
   - Increase revenue for your business
   - Get more high-quality leads to increase your sales
   - Get more traffic to your website
   - Establish your thought leadership in your industry
   - Being more successful with your search engine optimization efforts
   - Reduce your marketing cost
   - Increase your brand's social media engagement

2. Defining key performance indicators (KPI)

You should not only define the goals you wish to accomplish but also how you would measure the success of your content marketing strategy in achieving those goals. These KPIs will help you set the milestones you want to achieve.

These KPIs will help you effectively track the return on investment (ROI). Some of the KPIs for your content are as follows:

- Total monthly visitors to your website.
- The number of marketing qualified leads generated in a month from different channels.
- The bounce rate of your website.
- The total number of your website keywords on the first to third position, the number of website keywords on fourth to tenth positions in Google search results.
- The number of deals closed from your organic traffic.
- The total number of subscribers or followers on your social media channels.

3. Define your target audience

Your analytics will give you an insight into your target audience in a more precise way. Initially, you can start by creating buyer personas. You can describe the traits of your ideal customers and their online behavior.

The buyer persona is the starting point to target your audience. You need to evaluate whether you are targeting the right audience after every quarter by gaining insights from the analysis of your data.

In my personal experience, I have worked on a website that was getting 100,000 visitors per month. Even with a good visitor count for a niche industry, the deals were low. When we audited the website and looked at the keywords as well as data, we learned that approximately 50 percent of the traffic was made up of students who were coming just to get information. The issue was resolved by using more relevant keywords to derive traffic.

One of the critical factors in targeting the right audience is using the right keywords.

4. Audit your existing content

Most probably, as a business, you already would have a website and various social media channels. You need to audit all the existing content and marketing collaterals to analyze your current market position.

You can use an Excel to log all the URLs of your blog posts. Analyze all the page titles and descriptions and the page titles and descriptions of your pages that are visible in Google search results. A good page title and description help to get more clicks.

You need to audit all the content created with your brand name. You need to find out whether your content is aligned with your content marketing strategy. If your content is not aligned with your content marketing strategy, you will have to repurpose your old content by editing it or create new content that is aligned with the strategy.

5. Analyze your content distribution channels

Some channels are more suitable for a particular industry. For example, if you are in the business of home decor, an Instagram account and Pinterest board will be a more appropriate channel for your content rather than LinkedIn.

If you are operating in a niche industry such as SaaS (Software as a Service), you can use your blogs as a medium to distribute your content. A LinkedIn account will help you generate more leads.

If you are not sure about which channels are suitable for your business, then you can analyze your competitors and find out which channels they prefer.

6. Determine the content type you will create

There is an evolution of different content formats. The more content formats you include in your content marketing strategy, the more you will increase your reach.

The following are different content formats.

Blog Posts

This is the most effective content format to attract traffic to your website. A blog post that is optimized for the right keywords for search engines can get your potential customers to your website quickly.

A well-researched blog post, which is 1,000–2,000 words in length and gives a unique insight to the readers, will help you build a blog subscriber base. You can also share blog posts on different social media platforms such as Facebook, LinkedIn, and Twitter.

E-books

E-books are usually detailed and are published less frequently. E-books are a good way to get more leads for your business. You can create a separate landing page for your e-books and ask the page visitors to provide their e-mail address to download the e-book.

E-books are a great way to give valuable insights and detailed information to your blog readers. They not only help you establish your brand's thought leadership but also can act as a lead magnet.

If you are finding it difficult to write a complete e-book, then you can use your old related blog posts to compile an e-book. You will have to rewrite the old blog posts in a bid to make the content 100 percent plagiarism-free.

Case Studies

Case studies are the most important marketing collateral you can ever have on your website. While testimonials are credibility-building elements on your website, case studies take it to the next level by formulating a story that helps to build trust in your brand among your audience.

Case studies let other potential customers know how your business helped your customers. Even if you are into selling gift cards online, a good story will help your website visitors know how you are creating special moments for your customers.

You always need to have two types of content on your website: one which tells about the benefits of choosing your offering and another would be creditability building content. Your website visitors should easily know what you offer and how they can trust you. Case studies are an answer to how can they trust you. Case studies can be in a web page format as well as pdf format for your customers to download.

Templates

A template is a content format that your website visitors can use. For example, a content audit template that can be used by anyone to audit their website content. You can offer templates relevant to your business.

Infographics

Infographics are a mix of text and visuals. They are very effective for social media engagement, and you can add infographics to your blog posts to reduce the bounce rate (the number of visitors leaving your website after visiting just one page). You can find a lot of free tools to create infographics online.

Videos

Videos are the coolest thing, as YouTube has become the second most popular search engine after Google. Videos engage users who don't have time or patience to read your blog posts.

Videos also tend to get more shares as compared to a blog post on social platforms. You can use product explainer videos to describe your offerings. A 60-second product explainer video can engage your website visitors more easily.

Podcasts

Podcasts are used to stream audio content for your website visitors. The good thing about podcasts is that someone can listen to the podcast on the go. One-third of the total population in the United States has listened to at least one podcast. You can use podcasts to air interviews with some experts or your customers to give insights.

Social Media Posts

Different social media channels allow you to engage with users in different content formats. Some of the most used social media channels for business are:

- Instagram
- Twitter
- Facebook
- Pinterest
- LinkedIn
- YouTube
- Snapchat

You need to create a business page on different social media platforms. These social media platforms give you a great distribution channel to distribute your website content and create social engagements. Social media channels allow you to engage with your audience on a personal level.

7. Publish and manage content

You need to have an editorial calendar to publish your blog, your social media content, and sending out e-mails. You need to decide on the number of blogs you will publish on your website in a month. Select specific days of the week to publish blogs on your website.

One blog per week is acceptable, but if you are publishing two to three blogs in a week, it will be better if your site is relatively new, and you want to get more traffic on your website.

For your social media channels, you can take leverage of special days such as Friendship Day and Thanksgiving Day to make a connection with a personalized campaign.

You need to send out an e-mail to your blog subscribers to inform them about new blogs on your website. Sending out an e-mail to your blog subscribers every two weeks with your recently published blogs will be good to create engagement.

E-mail marketing is useful for nurturing your leads. It should be integral to your content marketing strategy.

8. Monitor your KPIs

When you start executing your content marketing strategy, you need to monitor the results. Google Analytics will help you monitor the KPIs of your content. In Chapter 6, you will learn how to set up a Google Analytics account and track the conversion goals you set up for your website.

Monitoring your KPIs will let you know that you know which content is working in your favor and which content is not working for you and what changes you need to make in your content strategy.

Some content marketing ideas from big brands:

Here are some successful content marketing examples, from some of the well-established brands.

Blogging Example

HubSpot offers a marketing automation tool that provides full-suite services to digital marketers. In its blog posts, HubSpot gives digital marketers some in-depth insights on topics such as e-mail marketing, content marketing, social media marketing, and much more.

It also offers e-books to its website visitors. In addition to a well-executed blogging strategy, HubSpot has also established an academy for learning and offering certifications.

Social media marketing examples:

Netflix India wished its users on friendship day 2019 in a unique way by tweeting "This Friendship Day, remember to wish the person you've never met whose account you're using." They used humor to grab the attention of the millennial population who are used to sharing their Netflix login credentials with their friends. They got 1,200 retweets in a couple of hours, which helped in creating a viral effect.

Glossier, which is into skincare and beauty products, cleverly utilized user-generated content to boost its brand on Instagram. Glossier reposted a compliment one of its fan posted on its Instagram page. The best part about using user-generated content is that it saves your time and resources required to create content.

Intrepid Travel is the world's largest small-group adventure travel company. It has its own guest posting content hub called "Journal." Travelers can share their experience and travel stories in Journal. This allows the brand to connect with its audience on a personal level. The travelers can also post their travel images on their Facebook page. This helps Intrepid to get over half a million followers on its Facebook page.

This strategy of user-generated content brings your brand closer to your target audience. It also helps you to get fresh user-generated content rather than you investing time in generating content.

AARP, which is America's biggest consumer magazine, decides which topics to cover in their magazine from the letters, social media posts, and e-mails it receives from its readers.

This is a great way to do content planning and creating a higher level of user engagement. The more you listen to your target audience, the more ideas you will get to feed your content production. AARP is a great example of using customer feedback to cater to their needs.

Zomato is a very popular app to find restaurants and used in around 24 countries. Zomato uses food images along with a pinch of humor to create engaging content. Its approach has made it very popular across social media platforms, which have resulted in increasing a large number of followers. Its visually appealing content helps it in achieving its conversion goal, which is to get more downloads of its mobile app.

Zendesk has one of the coolest approaches to target audience searching for Zendesk alternatives. It created a mini-site with the name Zendesk alternative and optimized a video around the keyword. This way, Zendesk not only gained a lot of new visitors to its brand but also earned goodwill for its wits.

Content Planning for Inbound Sales Funnel

You need to map your content as per the different stages of the customer journey. The stages of customer interaction with your brand are as follows:

- Awareness
Inbound marketing starts with creating awareness of the brand. The awareness stage of the customer journey is where people are looking for answers, resources, and insights that are helpful to them.

At the awareness stage, one of the most powerful content strategies is to create highly informative blog posts, e-books, and white papers. The purpose of this content would be to give insights that are unique and provides value to the target audience. At this stage, you will need to map your content with the keyword strategy for search engine optimization.

For example, a travel-planning agency starts creating blog posts on preparing the itinerary for popular destinations among its target audience. These blogs give readers insights on the must-visit places, the must-do activities, and the must-try out food at popular destinations.

• Interest

At the interest stage of the customer journey, the people are aware of the brand and interested to learn about the benefits they would get from the product or services.

As you have already created brand awareness to draw interest in your brand, you need content that tells about your brand benefits. You can also provide content that compares your brand with that of your competitors. You can provide content such as expert guides, webinars, and white papers that compare your brand features with your competitors.

E-mail marketing would work best at this stage of the customer journey. You can build a list of subscribers from your blog. You can start rolling out e-mails on a bi-weekly basis with your latest blog post along with communicating your brand benefits.

We can refer to the same example of the travel agency running a blogging campaign. As they build their subscriber base, they can start with e-mail marketing campaigns wherein they communicate the latest blogs on popular destinations along with information about how the travel agency can plan a visit to a particular destination. The call to action in the e-mail marketing campaign can be booking a call with the travel advisor from the agency.

• Desire

Your target audience is aware and interested in your brand. Now they are seeking information about the credibility of your product or services.

In the next stage of the customer journey, you would want to create a desire to purchase through your content. This can be achieved through the product and feature pages on your website. Case studies play an instrumental role in helping people making the purchase decision. Case studies tell your target audience how you have created value for your customers.

You will now be aware of the role of the feature/product pages on your website. In the customer journey, the website's main pages help to create the desire in the target audience to opt for your brand.

If we refer to the same example of the travel agency, they can have testimonials from the travelers who have opted for their services. Positive reviews from the customer also help in creating a desire for potential customers.

- Action

The customer at this stage has decided to go for your brand and takes the action of making the purchase. This is the stage where there is a potential for repeat sales and building engagement with the customer.

At this stage, you see the call-to-action buttons such as Buy Now, Get Started, Free Trial, Book Demo, and Talk to Sales. The most important content would be product literature, case studies, demos, and product explainer videos.

Free Trial is the most effective way to get users onboard and later ask them to go for a paid version. Most of the companies capitalize on free trials such as Netflix, Amazon Prime, and Zapier.

In the travel agency example, the content for the action stage could be scheduling a call with the travel advisor. They can place the "Talk to Us" call-to-action button in between their blog posts or at various places in their content.

Points to Remember

1. Digital marketing is, instead, a means to distribute your content to the right target audience effectively.
2. A content marketing strategy is a strategic approach to creating and distributing content for a specific target audience to make them take the desired action.
3. You need to ensure that all different channels and mediums where your content is available should have an underlying theme.

4. Creating a brand identity will help you stand out from the clutter of the competition.

5. A documented content marketing strategy will help you measure your effectiveness in achieving the goals you set forth.

6. Steps to create a content marketing strategy:
   - Define the goals you wish to achieve for your business
   - Define Key Performance Indicators (KPI)
   - Define your target audience
   - Audit your existing content
   - Analyze your content distribution channels
   - Determine the type of content you will create
   - Publish and manage content
   - Monitor your KPIs

7. Map your content as per different stages of the customer journey.

8. The steps of customer interaction with your brand are:
   - Awareness
   - Interest
   - Desire
   - Action

Assignment

1. Create a list of different content types and the distribution channels you would want to execute your content marketing strategy.

2. Create a content marketing strategy.

3. Prepare an editorial calendar to publish different types of content for the next three months.

4. List down the top three Key Performance Indicators you want to measure.

CHAPTER 4

Search Engine Optimization

In digital marketing, the most important goal for your brand will be that your website is discoverable by the maximum number of people you have chosen as your target audience online. Search engines act as a bridge between your website and your target audience.

What Is SEO?

Search engine optimization (SEO) is done to maximize the number of visitors on your website by ensuring your website content appears on top search results in search engines such as Google, Bing, Yahoo, and so on.

For example, you have a cake shop, and you have written an article on the chocolate cake recipe on your website. Through search engine optimization, you will be able to make your website appear in top search results in Google. This way, people interested in chocolate cakes will land on your site. In a nutshell, search engine optimization is done to increase the visibility of your website in search engine results.

Search engine optimization can be categorized into three different streams.

On-page SEO

On-page optimization is done on your website. The content you publish on your website and the keywords you optimize your content for. On-page involves optimization of content, the title of the pages, meta description of the pages on your website.

Off-page SEO

The off-page activities are not done on your website. These are mainly link building activities you do to build the credibility and authority of your website by getting backlinks from other high-authority websites. Off-page activities go beyond creating links for your website but also include social media marketing, PR, reviews, and user-generated content.

Technical SEO

Technical SEO is associated with the infrastructure of the website. It is done to optimize the website for the crawling and indexing phase. Technical SEO mainly includes the site structure, navigation, URL structure, website speed, mobile responsiveness, and any other technical aspects of the website.

Local SEO

Local SEO refers to optimizing your content to appear in local searches. For example, you are in Times Square in New York, and you search for the keywords "Coffee shops near me." You will get all the website pages of the coffee shops that are optimized for local search in Times Square.

SEO is mainly done to appear in organic results in the search engine. Organic results are those results for which you don't have to pay to rank in the search results, while inorganic results are the paid advertisements you see in search result pages.

This is why SEO is useful for small businesses and starts ups with small marketing budgets as SEO helps to build brand awareness and get customers at virtually no cost.

Let's explore each of these optimization techniques.

On-page SEO

Here is the list of activities you need to do for on-page optimization.

Keyword Research

The first step in on-page optimization is to find out the keywords your target audience is using to search for information on a product/service in the search engines.

The success of your SEO largely depends on the right keywords. Earlier the search engines gave preference to the content, which has precisely matching keywords. As Google keeps updating its algorithm to provide users the most relevant content, now the preference is given to the content that matches the search intent of the users, which is depicted through the keywords.

The user can search to find some information or to locate a website or buy a product.

There are three types of keywords based on search intent:

- Transactional keywords
- Informational keywords
- Navigational keywords

Transactional Keywords

Transactional keywords are those keywords that show the intent is to buy or purchase something. Some of the transactional keywords are:

- Buy
- Purchase
- Discount
- Download
- Free Trial

Informational Keywords

These are the keywords one uses to search for some information. Some of the examples of informational keywords are:

- How to
- What is
- Best ways
- Tutorial

Navigational Keywords

These are the keywords people use to search for a website of a famous brand. The user is typically aware of the brand, and they are using the keywords to navigate to the brand's website. Some of the navigational keywords are

- Testimonial
- Reviews
- Cost or Pricing

Now, as you know what the types of keywords used in the search engine are, you need to find the actual search terms that your target audience enters in the search terms.

With these keywords, you will be able to formulate your content marketing strategy, especially your blogging strategy. From the search terms, you will get the topics you have to write on to get relevant traffic (visitors) on your website. With the right and relevant keywords, you will not only increase the number of visitors on your website, but you will also increase the percentage of visitors who will buy from your website.

Finding Topics

The first thing is to list all the topics that are related to your website. For example, let's say you are a tour operator that plans adventure trips. Some of the topics that will be relevant to your business would be:

- Adventure treks
- Hitchhiking destinations
- White water rafting
- Bungee jumping
- Paragliding
- Camping sites

These are merely a broad category of topics but not keywords. Now you want to find the keywords that are used in the Google search engine. Just go to Google.com and type in "Adventure treks" and don't hit enter. You will see a list of suggestions such as "Adventure treks Alaska." These suggested keywords are used by a large number of people in Google.

You can use this strategy for all the topics you have selected. You should also search for these topics in the YouTube search bar as its now the second largest search engine.

Search-Related Keywords

Now use the same keyword "Adventure treks" in Google and search for the results. On the search results page, you will find a list of keywords at the bottom in "Searches related to Adventure treks."

Searches related to Adventure treks are the following:

- Adventure treks Yellowstone
- Adventure treks Alaska
- Adventure treks California
- Adventure treks jobs
- Adventure treks reviews
- Adventure treks RV checklist
- Adventure treks instructors
- Adventure treks LLC

Now you will have a list of keywords, but these still are not the keywords you will use.

Keywords Tool

Now you have a list of probable keywords; you need a keyword tool to find out the right keywords. You can use Ubersuggest to find the average monthly searches of a keyword for a specific location (Figure 4.1).

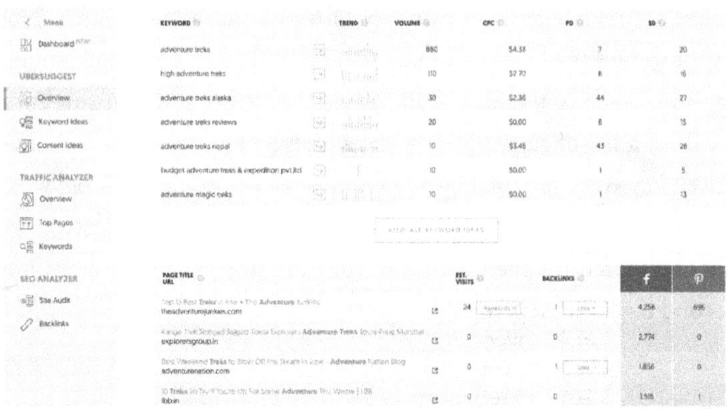

Figure 4.1 Keywords tool

For the keyword "Adventure treks" in the United States, Ubersuggest is giving a search volume of 880 with a SEO difficulty score of 19. It is important to note that not only the search volume but also the SEO difficulty is an important criterion to select the keyword. The SEO difficulty helps you to know the level of competition on the keyword.

A keyword with greater SEO difficulty means it would be challenging to rank on that keyword as already many websites are competing for getting in the top results.

Google Keyword Planner is another free tool for keyword research and planning, as this keyword tool gives you more accurate information than any other tool. The only drawback of using this tool is that it is more suitable for Google Ad campaigns rather than organic SEO.

Ahrefs is a paid tool and one of my favorites. Its "Keyword Explorer" gives you all information you need in a single interface. This tool gives you not only global search volume but also the keyword ranking difficulty and keyword ideas by the search volume.

The more the search volume on a keyword and lower is the keyword ranking difficulty, the more promising the keyword would be for your brand.

Keyword Difficulty

Always remember that as there is competition for your business offline. Similarly, you will face competition online in the search engines. If you have a good strategy, you can easily find the gaps in your competitors' strategy and take advantage of it.

If you have a new website, then you will have to build the credibility of your website to appear in top results. Until then, you should focus on less competitive keywords.

Some of the less competitive keywords are long-tail keywords. Long-tail keywords are four+ word phrases that have particular search intent. For example, the keyword "rent an apartment under 1000 dollars," might have very few, 100–200 searches a month, but they are very less competitive. You will be able to cover a lot of keywords through your long-tail keywords.

I have executed an online keyword strategy with long-tail keywords. I initially wrote a blog for a long-tail keyword, and the blog started giving ranking for the selected long keyword. Eventually, the blog started ranking for three- and two-word keywords, which were very competitive. In my experience, I don't think that long-tail keywords are not effective in bringing in traffic to the website. In the longer run, these keywords will be the most powerful arsenal in your online strategy.

Keyword Selection Criteria

Now, I provide you with the search criteria to select keywords:

1. High search volume
   The keyword should have a high search volume (high search volume depends on the chosen industry. For a niche B2B industry search volume of 1,000 may be called high whereas a search volume for the e-commerce search volume of 10,000 may be considered high).

2. Keyword difficulty
   Select the keywords with low keyword ranking difficulty if your site is relatively new and has low DR (Domain Rank). Domain Rank can be found using Ubersuggest or Ahrefs; the Domain Rank is on a scale of 1–100. The higher the DR, the higher the chances are for a keyword to rank. DR depends on your off-page activities, which include getting relevant backlinks from other high authority websites.

   A site that has high authority can go for medium to high difficulty keywords with good search volume.

3. Filter the keywords

This depends on the needs of your business. Even if the keywords you select have high search volume and less competition, but if it doesn't relate to your business, then you will not get higher sales despite getting higher traffic.

Let's refer to the previous example; you offer adventure treks through your website. You have selected a keyword as "flight booking," which has a high search volume. Although it may be a highly searched keyword as your site doesn't offer flight booking services, this keyword will not be fruitful for your business. A keyword such as "adventure gear" would be a right keyword as someone who is searching for adventure gear would want to go on an adventure trek. They would be lucky to find your website as you offer adventure trekking services.

4. Keyword trends

Google Trends is another useful tool to find out the keyword trends. You will be able to find the search trends related to any topic.

Implementing On-Page SEO

Now you have selected the keywords; the next step would be to start executing your SEO strategy.

Let's say you have written a blog on "Adventure Trek Destinations." You will learn how you should optimize your blog. All the optimization can be done through your WordPress CMS. Login to your website admin account. Usually, if the domain name of the site is abc.com, then your WordPress admin can be logged into by abc.com/wp-admin. You can use the Yoast Plugin with WordPress for on-page optimization (Figure 4.2).

1. Optimize the URL

The URL that will be created for the blog should have the selected keyword in the URL. In the above case, adventure trek destinations. For example, the URL can be https://yourwebsite.com/blog/bestadventuretrekdestinations

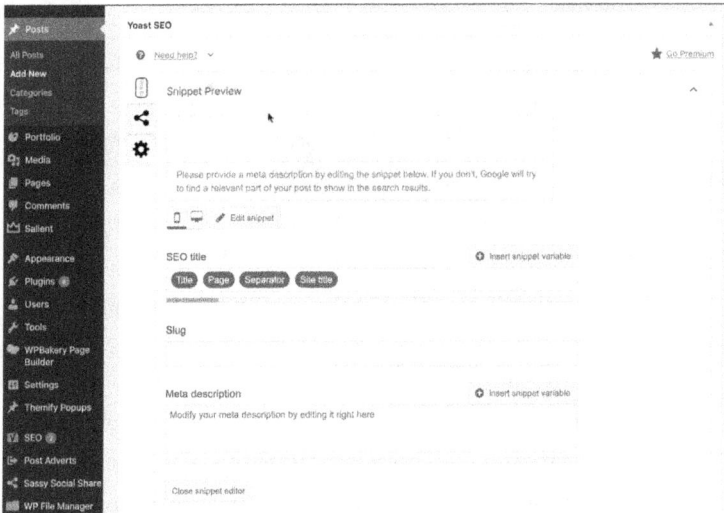

Figure 4.2 Implementing on-page SEO

2. Optimize the title tag

The title tag text will be visible in the search results. Whatever you write in the Title and Description tag will be visible in the search results. For example,

Best Adventure Trek Destinations: 15 must-visit treks

Your keyword should be closer to the beginning of your title tag. You should also use modifiers such as "2019," "best," "guide," "review," "checklist," as well.

3. Use H1 tag for blog title

You should use the H1 tag for your blog post title, which should have your selected keyword. Usually, most CMS such as WordPress use the H1 tag for the blog post title. You can use the Yoast Plugin with WordPress to set your title tag.

4. Use multimedia

Using multimedia such as charts, graphics, images, and videos increases the engagement of the visitor with the blog. Multimedia increases the time spent by users on your blog page. It also reduces the bounce rate, which is the percentage of visitors who navigate away from the site after viewing just a single page. A high bounce rate is not suitable for your website.

5. Use H2 tag for subheadings

   Use your chosen keyword in H2 subheadings at least once. Your blog post should have H2 and H3 tags, which tells Google that there are subtopics in your blog posts, which means a better content structure.

6. Use your keyword in introduction paragraph

   Your keyword should appear in the first 100 words of your blog post. The earlier your keyword appears, the better. We tend to miss out on the keyword in our introductory para; this is not a right approach when it comes to SEO.

7. Mobile-friendly pages

   Google prefers the sites, which are mobile-optimized, and it penalizes the sites that are not mobile optimized in the search results. By mobile responsive design, it means that your website is readable and looks good on the mobile screen.

8. Add some outbound links

   The outbound or external links in your blog helps Google to know which are the topics your blog post is related to. Linking out to external high-authority sites helps to build the credibility of your website. You add a hyperlink to any external article on any word or phrase in your blog.

9. Do internal linking

   Use some internal links by adding hyperlinks on words or phrases to your existing blogs. The internal links should appear early in your blog posts. Internal links help to bring down the bounce rate as well. A good number of internal links will be two to five inside your blog posts.

10. Ensure fast loading of website

    Make sure that your website takes less than four seconds to load. You can use a Content Delivery Network (CDN) to facilitate fast loading. Compress the images on your website to reduce the loading speed.

11. Use LSI keywords

    LSI keywords are those keywords that appear in searches related to your keyword. In our example where we used the keyword adventure trek, then the LSI keywords are adventure treks Yellowstone, adventure treks Alaska, adventure treks California, and so on.

12. Do image optimization

    The images in your blog post should include the keyword you select in the name of the image. You should also use the keyword in the Alt Text of the image. All the images in your blog post should have the target keywords and LSI keywords in the image name and Alt Text as well.

13. Include social sharing buttons

    Getting social shares of your blog post gets you to get more attention to your blog post. The social sharing buttons help your blogs getting distributed on social networks. The social-sharing buttons with a counter to show how many times your post was shared on a social network builds the credibility of your blog post.

14. Use long-format content

    Google prefers articles that are longer and are well researched. Usually, an article that is 2,000 words longer will have a higher chance of ranking on the search engines as compared to shorter blogs.

    A 1,000-word blog is reasonably good enough, but to impress Google, you need to push further and aim to write 2,000 words blog post.

15. Increase the time spent on your blog

    The more visitors are spending time on your blog post, the better it is perceived by Google. If visitors leave your blog post early, then Google will perceive it as low-quality content. Add engaging images, ppts, or videos to increase the time spent by the visitor on your blog.

16. Comments

    The more the number of high-quality comments on a blog post, the better the rankings it will get. Comments represent user engagement with the content. If people are commenting on your blog post, it means something is exciting and thought-provoking written on your blog posts.

17. A good Click-Through Rate

    Let's stick with our example with the keyword Adventure Treks. You have optimized the title tag of your blog post with "Best Adventure Trek Destinations: 15 Must-Visit Treks." This will be visible in the search results when some searches for Adventure Treks keyword. As you have written a blog exactly on 15 must-visit adventure trek destinations, anyone who clicks on your search result in the search engine will find the right information on your blog. This will result in a good Click Through Rate.

If you have not properly written the Title Tag and Description, the search results will turn off the visitors who will not click on your content. Ensure to get a good CTR; you need to spend some time on creating crisp Title and Descriptions to get more traffic on your blog posts.

18. Keyword density

The keyword density is the percentage of the number of times a keyword appears on a web page concerning the total number of keywords on the page. The keyword density should not be beyond 2.5 percent.

Keyword Density = (Number of times Keyword appears/Total number of words) * 100

Let's take an example that your keyword "adventure treks" appear 15 times in a 1,200 words blog post then:

Keyword density= (15/1200) * 100= 1.25

You can increase the keyword density to 2 percent in your blog, but it should look natural and not as that you have stuffed keywords.

Initially, people use to stuffed keywords in their articles just to rank on the Google search engine. Now Google penalizes the articles where the keywords are unnecessarily stuffed at strange places.

Off-Page SEO

Let's first understand what off-page is. Let's say you want to buy a new electric car, but you are unaware which models are best in your budget range and which features you should have in your car. You decide to call your close friend Jim who is a sports car enthusiast and very well acquainted with car engines. Jim tells you that although he knows inside out of the latest cars running on petrol, he has not explored the electric models yet. He asks you to give his cousin Rony a visit at his car dealership as he sells electric cars.

Now, as you trust your friend Jim with his knowledge about cars and his expertise, you will give no second thought in visiting Rony's car dealership and buying an electric car from his showroom. This is because you trust Jim, and Jim has faith in Rony. You have no reason to doubt Rony.

Now let's understand how this example is relevant for off-page. Off-page SEO implicates gaining the trust of the search engines as your website is recommended by some high-authority websites. If Google Search Engine was at your place, and it trusts Jim's website as a high-authority website for everything you want to know about cars. If Jim is recommending users on his website to visit Rony's website, then Rony's website can be trusted for its information value and credibility.

Off-page activities are done outside of your website. It is also referred to as link building activities or backlinking. The link building activities are done to get backlinks to your site. The benefit of getting links from high authority websites that are relevant to your website will give you a boost in terms of search engine rankings.

For example, if your website offers sports gear, then getting links from a high-authority site that is dedicated to sports news will be beneficial for your website. If you are getting links to your sports gear offering website from a high authority website that publishes food recipes, then that link will not be beneficial for your website.

The vital point to remember is that you only get the benefit of the links if you get do-follow backlinks. The do-follow link means that the site, which is providing a link to your website, acknowledges your website's authority. In a do-follow link, the link juice is passed to the linked website. Link juice is the SEO benefit that you want to get.

A no-follow backlink is one where there is the only link, but the authority from the source site is not passed to the linked website.

Let's understand this with an example. You own a restaurant, and one of your specialties is Chinese food. A food blogger visits your restaurants and is intrigued by one of your dishes. The blogger runs a high-authority website with 100,000 monthly visitors.

He decides to write an exhaustive guide on Chinese cuisine and wants to cover your restaurant's dish in the article. He is kind enough to give a do-follow backlink to your website. Now the do-follow backlink means that your website will get the SEO benefit of the backlink. If it was a no-follow backlink, then the users from the food blogger's website will come to your website, but your website will not get an SEO benefit.

Off-Page SEO Techniques

Here are some of the strategies to get do-follow backlinks.

Comments

Earlier, leaving comments on a high-authority website was the easiest way to get backlinks. People abused this strategy, and Google decided to stop giving SEO benefits to any such irrelevant comments.

The right way of commenting for the right audience helps build relationships with the blog owner and other people who post their comments.

Forums

A forum for discussion such as Quora will help you get relevant do-follow backlinks. You can participate in discussions that are relevant to your offerings. You should create a profile and keep your website's backlink in the profile information, as well.

Guest Posts

This is the most prominent way to get do-follow backlinks. A lot of sites accept guest posts and offer do-follow backlinks. Just do a Google search for guest blogging website related to your industry. As your articles get published on the website and you get a do-follow backlink, it will be very beneficial for your SEO.

This approach can be used to focus on certain keywords that are very relevant for your website. You can get backlinks to your specific pages that are optimized for chosen keywords.

Broken Link Building

In a broken link building approach, you find a high-authority website relevant to your site. Use any free broken link finder tool to find broken links on the site. You can provide your relevant website content to replace the broken link. The benefit to the high-authority website with broken links will be that there will be less page not found errors on their website. Page not found or 404 errors are bad for a website in terms of SEO.

Brand Mentions

If people are mentioning your brand on social networks or any other discussion forums, a good amount of brand mentions will give a search engine crawler a signal that your brand is trustworthy and credible.

Social Bookmarking

Some of the popular social bookmarking sites are Reddit, StumbleUpon, and Digg. The social bookmarking sites store, organize, and manage bookmarks of web pages.

Technical SEO

Now I suggest the steps to do technical SEO.

1. Review your website sitemap
   Your website's site map tells the search engine about the structure of your site and helps them discover fresh content. You can create a sitemap through different free site map creation tools and submit your site map through Google Search Console (Figure 4.3).

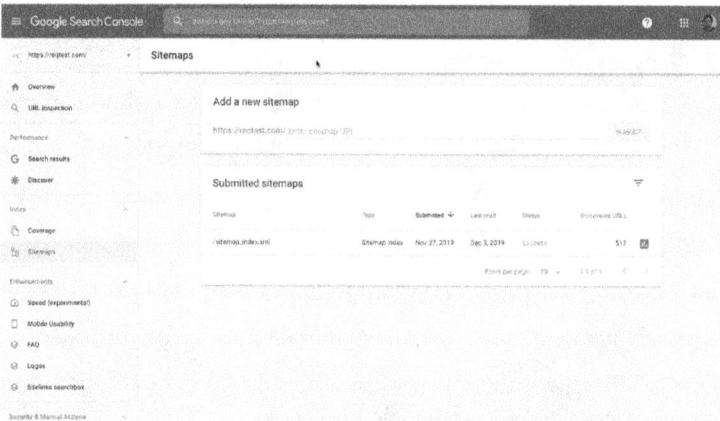

Figure 4.3 Review your website sitemap

Google and the Google logo are registered trademarks of Google LLC, used with permission.

Google Search Console is the free web service that allows webmasters to check indexing status and optimize visibility of their website. You can add your site maps through the Sitemaps tab in Google Search Console.

2. Review Indexing of your websites

You can check which pages of your website are indexed and which are not using Index Coverage Report in your Google Search Console. The number of pages indexed should be equal to the total number of pages on your website, minus the ones you don't want to get indexed.

3. Find the no-index pages

Find the pages that are blocked from indexing. The robots.txt file helps you to restrict pages from indexing.

4. Check the pages that are not internally linked

You need to check whether all pages are internally linked or not. The pages that are not internally linked are called orphan pages. You can find this information in Google Search Console. Ensure that all pages are internally linked, and there are no orphan pages.

5. Remove duplicate pages

Ensure there are no duplicate pages are there on your website. The pages with duplicate Title Tag and Description should be removed.

6. Check page speed

Ensure the page load speed of your website is good. You can use the PageSpeed Insights tool to check your website speed. It will also give solutions to improve page load speed.

7. Get your site re-crawled

Fix all the issues on your site; you can ask the search engine to re-crawl your website through Google Search Console.

Optimizing for Local SEO

- Setup up your Google My Business page.
- Add name, address, and phone number on all pages of your website.
- Get some reviews on Google Reviews
- Optimize your content for some keywords with your city or region included.

Points to Remember

1. Search engine optimization is done to maximize the number of visitors to your website by ensuring that your website content appears on top search results in search engines such as Google, Bing, and Yahoo.

2. Search engine optimization can be categorized into four different streams:
   - On-page SEO
   - Off-page SEO
   - Technical SEO
   - Local SEO

3. List of activities you need to do for on-page optimization:
   - Keyword research
   - Finding topics
   - Search-related keywords
   - Use Keywords tool
   - Find keyword difficulty
   - Discover keyword trends

4. Implementing On-page SEO
   - Optimize your URL
   - Optimize your Title tag
   - Use H1 tag for your blog title
   - Use Multimedia
   - Use H2 tag for subheadings
   - Use your keyword in introduction paragraph
   - The responsive design of the blog page
   - Add some outbound links
   - Do internal linking
   - Ensure Fast loading of website
   - Use LSI keywords
   - Do image optimization
   - Use long-format content
   - Increase the time spent on your blog

5. Off-page SEO

Strategies to get do-follow backlinks:
- Comments
- Forums
- Guest posts
- Broken link building
- Brand mentions
- Social bookmarking
6. Technical SEO checklist
   - Review your website sitemap
   - Review indexing of your websites
   - Find the no-index pages
   - Check the pages that are not internally linked
   - Remove duplicate pages
   - Check page speed

Assignment

1. Find out at least 10 new keywords for your website.
2. Write a blog for any one keyword and optimize the blog for search engines.
3. Create a backlink for the blog you have created.
4. Follow the same process for the remaining nine keywords.

CHAPTER 5

Social Media Marketing

Social media marketing brings in more traffic to your website and promote your products or services through social media platforms such as Facebook, LinkedIn®,[1] and Twitter.

Each social media platform is different and has a different impact. Social media marketing is a process of creating content in different formats and then distributing the content on various social media platforms to drive engagement and conversion.

Some social media platforms are good for sharing blogs, while some other social networks are suitable for sharing videos; some are good for sharing infographics. For each social media platform that you choose, you to have to create the content in the format that suits the social network.

If search engines were all about getting more traffic to your website, social media platforms are all about starting a conversation to build engagement with a maximum number of users.

The engagements you create through your social media channels should be authentic. Resorting to shady ways such as purchasing followers and likes, in the long run, lead to a negative image on social networks.

Influencer marketing on social media platforms has increased over the years. Now the users who have a large number of followers on social media platforms are getting paid for promoting a cause or a business.

The new-age influencers are not necessarily celebrities, but even if they have 30,000 to 40,000 followers, they can create a positive impact on social media for a brand.

Influencer marketing is dependent on the nature of your business and your target audience. For an FMCG brand, a large number of followers may be good, but for brands operating in the B2B domain,

---

[1] LinkedIn® professional networking services

only a few right connections on business networking platforms can be useful. A business can approach these "micro-influencers" to promote their brand on social media platforms to get higher brand visibility and engagement.

Let's take an example. You have a restaurant and you want to promote it through social media. You ask a very famous food blogger in your city to visit your restaurant and tweet a picture of their favorite dish from your restaurant. Let's say that the blogger has 40,000 followers on Twitter, and most of them live in your city. The blogger's tweet about their favorite food from your restaurant will reach a large number of followers. You can expect some food enthusiasts to visit your restaurant.

You can find these micro-influencers on social media for your business by searching for your industry-related topics. You can easily find some good micro-influencers who can be helpful in promoting your business on social media platforms.

Social media also plays a vital role in the buyer journey of a customer. Social networks help your brand to create a story that resonates with your target audience. The sales pitch has now been replaced by your brand story on social media platforms.

For example, Apple, rather than showcasing its product images on its Instagram page, posts the pictures clicked on iPhone by the users with a hashtag #ShotoniPhone. This is an excellent way for a brand to connect with its users on a personal level by letting them share what they are experiencing through pictures and videos.

The social media platforms also provide messaging platforms that give opportunities for people to reach out to a brand directly.

Apart from organic marketing, social media platforms allow you to run paid advertisements. You can very precisely target users on social media platforms based on their preferences and interests. Through your advertisements, you can reach the exact target audience on social media platforms.

Creating Your Social Media Strategy

You need to create a strategy for your social media marketing. Here are the steps to create your social media strategy.

1. Setting goals

   The first step is to set some measurable goals you want to achieve through your social media platforms. Some examples of social media marketing goal:

   - You want to gain 50,000 followers on Twitter, Facebook, and LinkedIn®.
   - You want to increase your sales by 10 percent through social media platforms.
   - You want to get a 15 percent higher social share of your blogs on social media platforms.

   Keeping realistic and measurable goals will help you identify the performance of your social media platforms.

2. Research your audience

   The next step would be to find out who you would want to target through your social media platforms. If you have a brand that sells sportswear, then you would want to target users who are actively engaged in sports.

   You also need to evaluate the social media platform best suited for your business. For example, a consumer product brand will find Facebook, Twitter, or Instagram more suitable to target their audience. A technology company offering Software as a Service (SaaS) platform will find LinkedIn® more suitable to target their audience.

   The best approach for the evaluation would be to do research on your competitors and the industry leaders. You need to know which social media platform your competitors are using, how many followers they have, what kind of content they are posting, and how often.

3. Identify the metrics you want to track

   As a social media platform is for engagement, you need to track the right Key Performance Indicators (KPIs) to track these engagements. Some of the metrics to follow are the following:

   Reach: This metrics gives you insight into the number of unique visitors that your post reached. This will help you to know how many people are viewing your post. Let's say you have posted a blog on your website and shared it on Facebook. You would like to track how many people on Facebook saw your blog post.

Clicks: The number of people who clicked on your social media posts gives you an insight on how compelling your posts are in driving action. The main goal of sharing your website blogs or pages on social media is to motivate people to click and land on your site.

Engagement: This metrics gives you insight into the total number of social interactions divided by the number of impressions. This is one of the most critical metrics you want to track as it tells how many people saw your post and out of it how many interacted with your post through like, comment, shares, or clicks. Higher engagement is necessary for higher brand recall.

Organic and Paid: You should track the performance of your paid ads on social media platforms along with organic (nonpaid) content performance. You can use organic social media marketing for different goals and paid ads for different purposes.

4. Create content calendar

Now, as you are aware of what goals you want to achieve, who are your target audience, who are your competitors, and how will you measure the performance of your social media platforms? The next step would be to create a content calendar with different types of content that you will create for different social media channels.

For example, you can outline the details, such as if you publish blogs on your website twice a week on Mondays and Wednesdays. Then you will be sharing these blogs on your social media channels on Tuesdays and Thursdays. You will share the blogs in relevant social groups on Fridays. You will create an infographic every Wednesday and will share it on Twitter. You will publish a blog on LinkedIn® biweekly every Monday. So this kind of content calendar will help you stick to your social media goals. You need to create a content calendar as per your social media goals.

5. Power of user-generated content-driven

The user-generated content is compelling for a brand in terms of engagement. Let's take an example that you are a toothpaste manufacturer. To gain traction for your brand on social media platforms, you decided to start a campaign where you ask your target audience to click photos of people and share them on Twitter with a hashtag

#sharingsmiles. People take notice of your campaign and start tweeting pictures of their friends and family smiling. This is an example of user-generated content that can boost your brand awareness and increase the number of followers on social media.

6. Start tracking performance

Every social media platform gives you insight into the different metrics. You need to track the performance of what you are posting on social media. Without monitoring the performance, you won't be able to know what changes you will have to make in your next posts.

You can personalize your message and can be informal in approaching your target audience through social platforms. You can be playful, humorous, sarcastic, and caring, or you can demonstrate any other personality trait of your brand on social networks.

There are numerous social media platforms on the Internet. Every social media channel has its purpose and a different kind of user base. Here we discuss the most powerful social media platforms that you can use for your business.

Facebook Ads

Investing in Facebook Ads can be one of the best decisions for your brand. You can create immense opportunities for your business through Facebook Ads. The reason Facebook Ads is so much useful is that it gives you a high level of customization, greater control, and precise targeting of the audience.

Facebook also allows you to run your ads on Instagram, as well. You can run an integrated campaign for both Facebook and Instagram through the Facebook Ads interface. The icing on the cake is that Facebook Ads are rather inexpensive than any other paid ads you run online.

Facebook Ads Manager

The Facebook Ads Manager is a very powerful tool. To start using Facebook Ads, you need to start with the following things.

Purpose of Your Facebook Ads

The first step would be to outline the purpose you want to run Facebook Ads. You have to list down the following:

- The product or services you wish to promote through your Facebook ads
- The ideal audience of your ads
- The target audience of your Facebook ads is at which stage in your inbound marketing funnel
- The pain points you will address in your ads
- The benefits of your product or service
- The goal you want to achieve through your Facebook ads
- The purpose of your Facebook ad, getting traffic on-site, brand awareness

Choosing the Objective

You can easily navigate to the Ads manager interface on Facebook by clicking on the blue drop-down button at the top right-hand side of the blue navigation pane on Facebook. Click on Manage Ads to open your Ad Accounts. As you click on your account name, it will take you to the page where you will find the Create button, which will allow you to create an Ad.

Facebook continuously changes its user interface to improve your user experience. There might be some changes to navigate to the ads interface page; you can easily find this information on the Facebook Help Center (Figure 5.1).

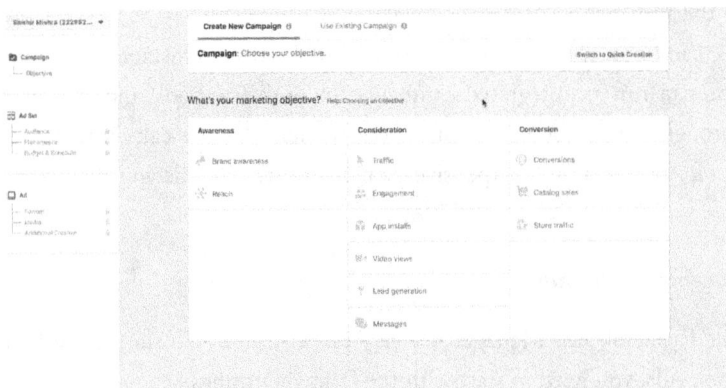

Figure 5.1 Choosing the objective

Facebook lets you choose the objective of your ad campaign. The objective is a vital part of Facebook as the ad optimization and placement are directly related to your objective.

There are the following three broad objectives in Facebook Ads:

- Awareness
  - Brand Awareness
  - Reach
- Consideration
  - Traffic
  - Engagement
  - App Installs
  - Video Views
  - Lead Generation
  - Messages
- Conversion
  - Conversions
  - Catalogue Sales
  - Store Traffic

Awareness

This objective helps to increase the brand awareness of your business. It is further divided into the following.

Brand awareness: This is to increase the awareness of your business, brand, or service.

Reach: This objective is to reach the maximum number of people you want to target.

Consideration

This objective encourages people to get interested in your business and seek more information. It is further divided into the following items:

Traffic: It is chosen when you want to drive traffic on a specific landing page or URL of your website.

Engagement: This objective is used when your main goal is to get more people to like, comment and share, or claim any offer.

App installs: This objective is chosen when you want people to download and install your app from the app store. You will include your app's exact download page on the App store.

Video views: The objective of video ads is to get as many people as possible to watch your brand's video.

Lead generation: This is the objective you choose when you want to generate leads for your business. The lead can be as simple as getting the business e-mail ids of people.

Messages: This is the objective you choose when you want to connect with your existing customers.

Conversions

This objective helps to get the people to buy your products or sign-up for trial of your service, and so on.

Conversions: This is the objective you choose when you want your website visitor to take a specific action. For example, the action could be to make a purchase, add items to the shopping cart.

Catalog sales: This objective is very useful for showcasing your e-commerce site's catalog to get more sales.

Store traffic: This objective can be chosen to get people to visit your physical store.

Choosing the right objective will help you achieve your goal. You can even do a split A/B testing of your Facebook ads by choosing different objectives.

Audience targeting: As you choose the objective of your ad, the next step would be to target the right audiences. You need to Create a New Audience or select the existing audience through Use Saved Audience in the next step. Alternatively, you can create audiences by clicking on Audiences in the shortcut (Figure 5.2).

There are three types of audience on Facebook:
- Custom Audience
- Lookalike Audience
- Saved Audience

You can create a Saved Audience with an Audience Name to reuse it for your Facebook ads. The Saved Audiences are those in which you can

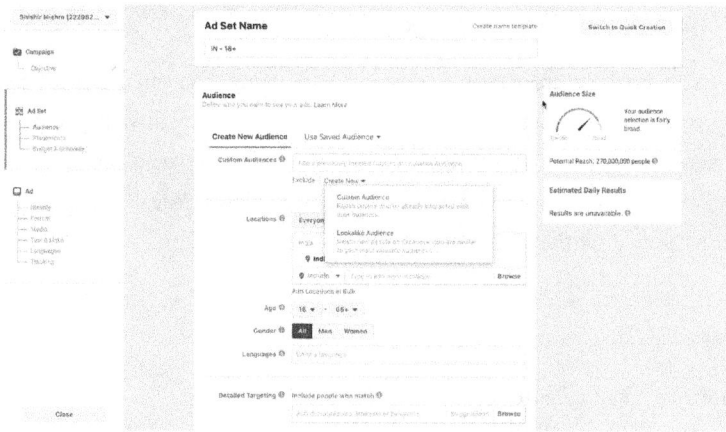

Figure 5.2 Audience targeting

target the audience based on their location, age, gender, used devices, income level, and so on.

The location-based targeting can be done on the following basis:

- Country
- State/Region
- Countries
- Designated Market Area (DMA)
- City
- Postal Code
- Specific Address Radius

There is another level of segmentation:

- Everyone in the location (Default): as per the user's last updated location
- People who live in this location: as per the user's Facebook profile information and confirmed based on their IP address
- People currently in this location: based on users' mobile device usage in a specific location
- People traveling to this location: users whose current location is this area and it must be at 100 miles away from their home location.

Demographic-Based Targeting

You can set the users' Age, Gender, and Languages. You can set a specified age range. You can set the Gender of the target audience as well. The Language setting is used when you are creating an ad in a particular language, and you want to target only the people who know the language. It is better not to set the language.

Detailed Targeting

Interests based (Figure 5.3)

This is the most interesting ad targeting feature you will get in Facebook ads. You can target people based on their interests. You can even target audiences who are interested in your competitors.

The interests are based on the Facebook pages the users have liked, the apps they use. You can target at a very detailed level using this feature.

Behavior based

Behaviors include your target audiences' purchase history, the events they like, their special occasions, and so on. Facebook collects this data through data analytics.

Now, let's take an example of how to create a Saved Audience. For example, let's say Rajesh owns a handicraft store in Connaught Place,

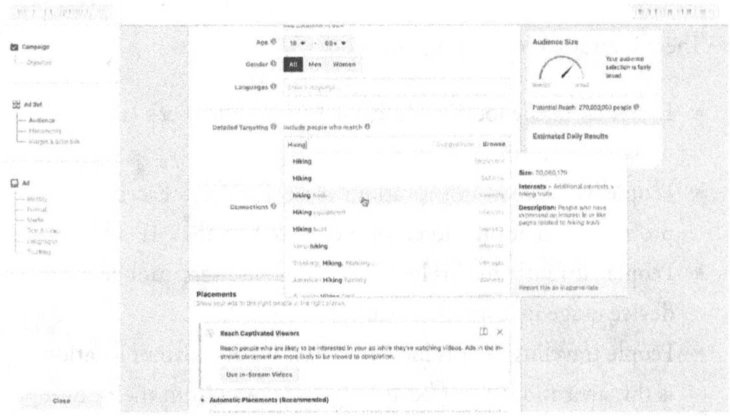

Figure 5.3 Interests based

New Delhi. It is a central market in New Delhi with high-street brands. He has a Facebook Page for his handicraft store. He wants to run a Facebook Ad to target Facebook users in a bid to get more store visits over the weekend.

He names this audience as Weekend Store Visitors. Now, as he wants to target people who are in his vicinity, he chooses the location as Connaught place and selects the option People recently in this location. He knows that usually, people in the age bracket of 35–70 years are more interested in his exquisite handicrafts items. He selects the Age range as 35–65+. He selects the Gender setting as all.

In the Detailed Targeting section, he selects the interest as "handicrafts," handmade accessories, Memento-Personalized Gifts.

Now he can use this Saved Audience every weekend to target people who are interested in handicraft items and are shopping in Connaught Place, New Delhi. You will see when you set all the filters, the number of target audiences decreases as the targeting gets more precise.

Custom Audiences

The Facebook custom audience is used for re-marketing activities. You can target your past website visitors or people who have any way engaged with your content.

There are different types of Custom Audience. Here I have discussed the Custom Audience that you can use for your business.

Customer List: You can add a list of e-mail ids, phone numbers, or even Facebook User ids to create a Customer List. For uploading a Customer List, you need to have a Business Account.

Engagement Custom Audience from Facebook sources: You can also create audiences of those who engage with your posts, videos, events, and forms on Facebook and Instagram. The engagements are tracked for the past 365 days.

Customer List Upload: You can export the list of e-mail contacts you want to target from your CRM tool and then upload a CSV file.

You can add multiple identifiers such as e-mail address, first name, country, year of birth, and so on. The more identifiers you add, it would be easier to target the Facebook users.

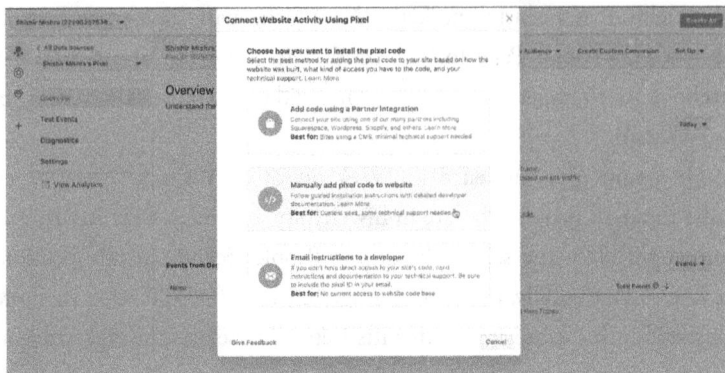

Figure 5.4 Website traffic

Website traffic (Figure 5.4): To target your website visitors on Facebook, you need to add a tracking code named as Facebook Pixel on your website. Click on Ads Manager on the top left-hand side, from the first column, that is, Manage Business, click on Events Manager. You will find a green button to Set up a Pixel code. Select the option manually add Pixel code to your website. You will find the pixel code. You can copy the pixel code and paste it to the header.php of your WordPress site.

Here are the steps to do it (Figure 5.5).

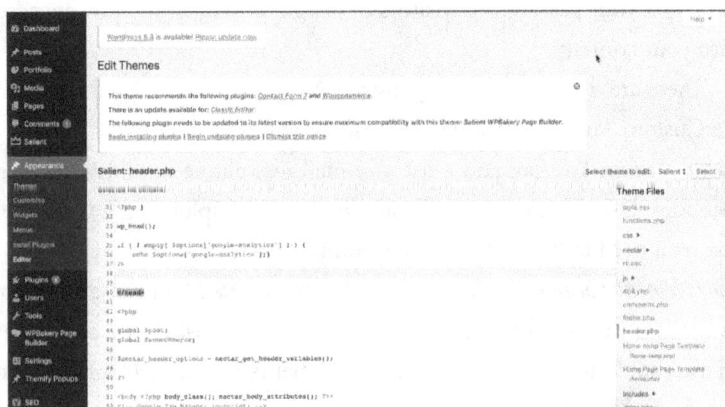

Figure 5.5 Adding pixel code to a WordPress site

1. Login into the Wp-admin account (for example, www.coffeebreak. com/wp-admin to login into admin account).
2. On the dashboard, you will find the Appearance tab on the left menu bar.
3. As you click on Appearance, you will find the Editor option. Click on Editor.
4. You will be navigated to the Edit themes page. Search for header.php using CTRL+F.
5. As you find header.php, click on it, and you will be allowed to edit it.
6. Look for the html tag</head> or use CTRL+F to find it.
7. As you find the tag </head>, click in front of it to paste the tracking code provided by Facebook.
8. Ensure your tracking code is in between <head> and </head> tags. Click on the Update File button.
9. Now you can wait for some time for the data to be available in your Facebook Ads account.

You can take the help of your website developer if you are using a website with some different CMS. You can also find some plugins to install Facebook Pixel on your website.

Now, as your pixel code is installed, you can navigate back to Ads Manager→Audiences→Create Audience→Custom Audience→Website Traffic.

You will find your pixel code appearing in Create a Website Traffic Custom Audience window. You can select the website visitors you want to target. You can target the visitors who have visited certain pages on your website. You can also select the basis of the time spent by visitors on your website.

You can target the most recent visitors to your website in the past 30 days. You can even choose to exclude a certain audience. You can name the audience and add a description of the audience.

Facebook Lookalike Audiences

The Facebook Lookalike audiences let you target audiences that are similar to your custom audiences who have a higher probability of converting. You can select the location of the audience as well as Select the Audience Size based on the percentage of the population.

Now you can start with creating advertisements through Ads Manager, Create Ad Campaigns. You can then choose where you want to display ads. You can choose the ads to appear on desktop only, mobile-only, or both mobile and desktop.

You can keep the placements as Automatic Placements, or you can Edit Placements to specify where you want your ads to appear.

Set a Budget

The next step would be to set the daily budget you want to spend on your Facebook Ads. You can set a lifetime budget or a daily budget for your ads based on whether you want to run your ads indefinitely or for a certain duration.

Select Your Ad Format

You can create ads for different formats on Facebook. You can select from

- Single image ads
- Video ads
- Carousel ads with several images or videos
- Canvas ads
- Collections

Choose the ad format that you think will get your highest engagement and more clicks. You should also provide the URL of your website where you want the ad viewers to land. Fill in all the details. A CTA button is important for a higher conversion rate.

The ad interface is very intuitive and gives you a lot of options to customize your ad. You can also preview how your ad will look to your target audience.

Monitor Ads

As you start running your ads, the next step will be to monitor the results. You will learn about the effectiveness of your ads. You need to watch out the cost per click (CPC). The relevancy score lets you know how much your ad is relevant to your landing page.

LinkedIn® Ads

LinkedIn® is a very powerful business-networking platform. It allows you to connect with your potential customers and the decision makers directly. LinkedIn® is more suited for business-to-business domains, whether you are a SaaS provider or you provide office furniture.

LinkedIn® gives you direct access to professionals around the globe. It provides a more formal business communication channel over Facebook or Twitter, which is more preferred for personal communication.

Creating LinkedIn® Ads

The first thing you need to run LinkedIn® ads is an active Company page. It's better you first start with creating engagements organically by actively posting on LinkedIn® to get a good number of followers.

You can use your company page as a medium to highlight the benefits of your offerings. You can regularly post your blog updates, company information, or any such thing that is more relevant to your business. LinkedIn® is considered a trustworthy source. Therefore, the promotional material is taken more seriously than any other place.

There are certain guidelines you need to follow before making your LinkedIn® pages. You will find all the requirements as you create your company page.

You can create Showcase pages as well, which you can use to showcase specific products. Such as Adobe uses its Showcase pages to highlight its products such as Adobe Create Cloud, and Adobe Document Cloud. Only use Showcase pages when you have a product or service that needs its page.

LinkedIn® Pay Per Click Advertising (Figure 5.6)

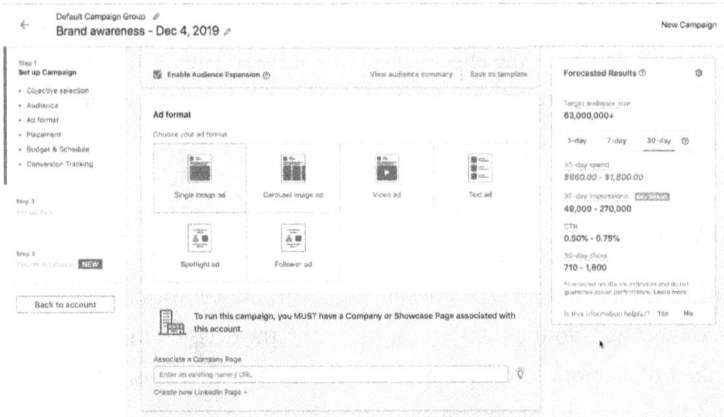

Figure 5.6 LinkedIn® pay per click advertising

Display and Text Ads

LinkedIn® provides users with PPC Ads display and text ads. The display and text ads give you an option to write a 25-character headline, 75-character description along with an image of 50 by 50 pixels. These ads are short ads that you can use along with your company logo to give an insight into what you offer. It is a short and crisp ad that you will find at different places on LinkedIn®.

Sponsored Content

The sponsored content gets highlighted in the prime places on LinkedIn®. This content appears in the news feed of your target audience. The sponsored posts get you more eyeballs and higher clicks, which leads to greater engagement. This content is great for lead generation.

Premium Display Advertising Types

The premium display ads on LinkedIn® differ in terms of size and placements of the ads. The four different formats of ads are as follows:

Medium Rectangle (300 × 250 pixels)

These display ads appear on the right-hand side of the pages. These ads appear on specific pages such as home, company, profile, and group pages.

Wide Skyscraper (160 × 600 pixels)

These are the tall ads that appear on the user's inbox and message pages.

Text link

These ads appear on the top of a page in text format with no image, and they appear on home, profile, company, group, and message pages.

Leaderboard (728 × 90)

These ads appear at the bottom of certain feeds as a landscape style image. These ads try to capture users' attention before the users leave LinkedIn®.

Sponsored InMail

This is one of the most powerful marketing tools to reach directly to the LinkedIn® inbox of your target audience. You can select a highly targeted group and send an e-mail message to them on LinkedIn®.

An e-mail has a higher conversion rate and remains one of the most effective ways to deliver your message.

Follow Company Ads

You can run ads to increase the number of followers of your LinkedIn® company page. You can target your followers without spending any money. As you start with your company page, your first conversion goal should be to increase the number of your followers.

Twitter Ads

Twitter is the best platform for creating brand awareness and getting people engaged with your brand. If you are active on Twitter, you might have come across promoted tweets. These promoted tweets appear in your news feeds. Twitter also provides you option to create Twitter Ad campaigns. Let's take a closer look at Twitter advertising:

Advertising Objectives

Twitter provides you with different objectives to choose from for your ad campaign (Figure 5.7).

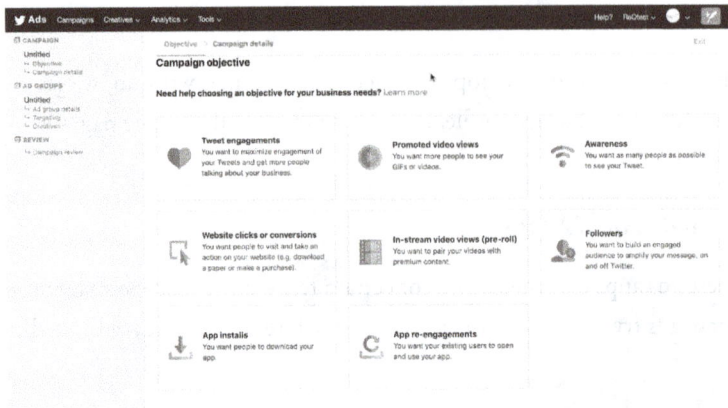

Figure 5.7 Twitter Ads

Tweet Engagements

This objective is well suited when you want to engage a maximum number of people with your tweets and start conversations related to your brand.

Promoted Video Views

You want more people to see your brand videos or gifs.

Awareness

This objective is great if you want your tweets to be viewed by as many people as possible.

Website Clicks or Conversion

You might want people to visit your website and make a purchase or start a free trial of your web application. This objective helps you get more people to visit and convert through your website.

In-Stream Video Views (pre-roll)

This objective will allow you to run your video ads before videos created by any popular publisher or video creators.

Followers

To increase the number of followers on your Twitter handle, you can choose this objective.

App Installs

You can choose this objective if you want people to download your app.

As you choose your campaign objective, you have to give a name to your campaign now, set a total budget, and schedule when you want to run the campaign.

Creating an Ad Group

The ad groups help you to segregate your campaigns, whether you want to do split testing or segregate the total campaign budget into different ad groups. You should choose the Bid Type as Automatic bid as it will enable Twitter to optimize your bid to get good results at a lower price.

Targeting

For targeting the right audience, you will have to select the right location, language, and device that you want to target. You can choose your target audiences from your followers based on some keyword, interest, behavior, or tailored audiences targeting. This is something similar to what you can do with Facebook Ads.

Creating Ads

Now the most important thing is your ad creative, which will help you to create engagement. You can choose an existing tweet to promote, or you can create a new tweet for your ad.

You now have to "Launch" your campaign.

Points to Remember

1. Social media marketing is a process of creating content that suits each social media platform to derive engagement.
2. The best part about social media platforms is that you can do a very precise targeting on social media platforms based on the preferences and interests of the users.
3. Creating your social media strategy
   - Goals setting
   - Research your audience
   - Identify the metrics you want to track
   - Start tracking performance
4. Facebook Ads give you a high level of customization, greater control, and highly accurate targeting of the audience.
5. There are following objectives of Facebook Ads
   - Brand Awareness
   - Reach
   - Traffic
   - Engagement
   - App Installs
   - Video Views
   - Lead Generation
   - Messages
   - Conversion
   - Catalog Sales
6. Audience targeting
   There are three types of Audience on Facebook
   - Saved Audience
   - Custom Audience
   - Lookalike Audience
7. LinkedIn® Ads
   LinkedIn® is more suited for business-to-business domains, whether you are a SaaS provider or you provide office furniture.

8. LinkedIn® Pay Per Click Advertising
   - Display and Text Ads
     - Premium Display Advertising Types
     - Medium Rectangle (300 × 250 pixels)
     - Wide Skyscraper (160 × 600 pixels)
     - Text link
     - Leaderboard (728 × 90)
9. LinkedIn® Sponsored Content
   - Sponsored InMail
   - Follow Company Ads
10. Twitter Ads

Twitter provides you with different objectives to choose from for your ad campaign.

   - Tweet engagements
   - Promoted video views
   - Awareness
   - Website clicks or conversion
   - In-stream video views (pre-roll)
   - Followers
   - App installs

Assignment

1. Select a social media platform most suitable for your business from Facebook, LinkedIn®, or Twitter.
2. Choose an objective for running your social media ad.
3. Create an ad campaign and run it for a week on business days.
4. Track the performance of your campaign.
5. Analyze the performance of your campaign in terms of your chosen objective.
6. List down three things you learned from running your ad campaigns.

CHAPTER 6

Google Analytics

Google Analytics is a free to use website analytics tool provided by Google that allows you to get insights into the visitors of your website. You get to know how people find your website over the Internet and how visitors interact with your website.

Why Use Google Analytics for Your Website?

As you create and execute your digital marketing strategy, you will need data analytics to monitor how is your digital marketing performance. Google Analytics lets you analyze your website data and the goals you wish to accomplish through your website. Let's explore why you need Google Analytics for your website:

1. How do people find your website?
   Google Analytics will let you know how people are landing on your website. It will help you to find out how the visitors find your website. Do most of your site visitors come through the search engine? Do you get more visitors through your links on the social media networks? Is there any other site where your website links are available? Is it your paid ads that drive maximum traffic? Or are people directly typing in your website URL in the browser? You can find this information in the Reports→Acquisition section.

2. Which actions are visitors taking on your website?
   Google Analytics will let you know what people are doing on your website. How they navigate through the site, which buttons they click, and which forms they submit? You also get to know how much time the visitors spend on a particular page. The Behavior section of Google Analytics is dedicated to these reports.

3. Which are the most popular pages on your website?

   With the help of Google Analytics, you will be able to learn which page of your website gets the most traffic (visitors). If your site has a specific goal, such as getting the e-mail address of the visitors, you can track which page of your website is contributing maximum to accomplish the goal.

4. Which type of visitors is coming to your website?

   Google Analytics will let you know what kind of visitors are coming to your website. You will get information on the demographics, geography, and online interest of the visitors. You will also get to know which devices are the visitors using to log in to your website.

   The information you get through Google Analytics helps you to analyze the performance of your digital marketing efforts. You can learn about the ROI of your online marketing. At a granular level, you can use the insights you get from Google Analytics to feed your digital marketing strategy.

   For example, a website renders different experiences on different browsers. If you are getting visitors through a browser where your site has a bad user experience, then most of the users will leave your website early. You can use this information to improve your website.

Knowing Your Google Analytics Account

Google Analytics is set up in such a way that the organization is the highest level; it usually represents a company or an enterprise. A company can have multiple Google Analytics accounts. Organization-level accounts are only suitable for large businesses that have a diverse portfolio of products. This is an optional level.

Account

This level of Google Analytics is mandatory, wherein you can have multiple accounts. You can create up to 50 properties in an account. For example, you are provided a Software as a Service (SaaS) to your customers. You have a website for selling the subscription of your software. You also have a help site for your software. You can have a single account wherein you can add both your website and your web app (software) as properties.

Property

A property can be a website or a web app. A property can support a maximum of 25 views.

View

A view can contain the filtered data from your website. You can have a filter on your IP address so that the traffic from your IP address doesn't land in Google Analytics. You should have two Views per property. One View should be of unfiltered data just in case a View is deleted; there is no way to recover your data.

Dimension and Metrics

It is essential to know how Google Analytics presents data to you. There are Dimension and Metrics, which is used to categorize data.

Dimension

Some of the examples of dimension are:
- Device
- Landing page
- Location
- Browser
- Customer type

Metrics

Some of the examples of Metrics are:
- Pageviews
- Conversions
- Bounce rate

- Sessions
- Session duration

Setting Up Google Analytics

The first step to getting insights is to set up a Google Analytics account for your website. You can use your Gmail account to set up your Google Account. If you don't have a Gmail account, you can create one.

As you login to the Google Analytics account, it will ask you information on the website you want to track and monitor. You need to provide details such as Account Name, Website Name, URL, Industry, and your Time Zone.

As you will fill in the details, you will be redirected to the page with an option "Get Tracking ID." You have to accept the Terms of Services then.

Setting Up Tracking

You will then get your Tracking ID and your Google Analytics tracking code. You can anytime get this code in the Admin Property Tracking info section.

You have to paste this tracking code on the website you want to track, and the code should be there on every page of your website. This is relatively simple to do if you are using a WordPress website. All you will have to do is paste your tracking code in the header.php file.

Here are the steps:

1. Login into the wp-admin account.
2. On the dashboard, you will find the Appearance tab in the left menu bar.
3. As you click on Appearance, you will find the Editor option. Click on Editor.
4. You will be navigated to the Edit themes page. Search for header.php using CTRL+F.
5. As you find header.php, click on it, and you will be allowed to edit it.
6. Look for the Html tag</head> using CTRL+F (Find function)

7. As you find the tag </head>, click in front of it to paste the tracking code provided by Google Analytics.

8. Ensure your tracking code is in between <head> and </head> tags. Click on the Update File button.

9. Now you can wait for some time for the data to be available in your Google Analytics account.

If you don't have a WordPress based site, you can take the help of a developer. The process to paste the Google Analytics tracking code on your website is simple. You can find steps to paste the tracking code on your website through the Google search engine.

Setting Up Conversion Goals

After you set up the tracking code on your website, the next most crucial step would be to set up the conversion goals. You have created your website for a specific goal. For example, your goal is to get more people to sign up as subscribers and provide their e-mail id. By setting up the conversion goal, you will be able to find out how effectively you are achieving your goals through your website.

Create a New Goal

1. Click on the Admin tab (Settings icon) at the bottom left of your Google Analytics home screen; you will get three columns on the page, namely, Account, Property, and View.

2. Under the third column that is, View column, you will find Goals. Click on "Goals."

3. On the Goals page, click on the +New Goal button (Figure 6.1).

4. You will then find a Goal setup option, select the Custom option, and click on Continue.

5. Now you will be prompted to provide the name of your goal and choose the type of the goal. You should provide names relevant to your goal, for example, Sign-up, Free Trial, Subscribers, and so on. This will help you remember the conversion you are tracking. As

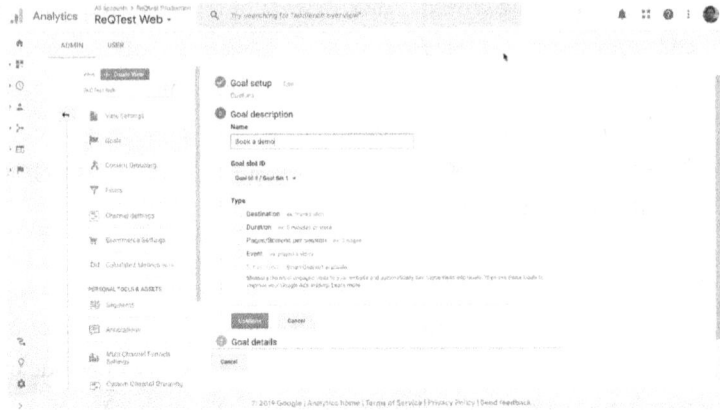

Figure 6.1 Create a new goal

Google and the Google logo are registered trademarks of Google LLC, used with permission.

you name the Goal, Select Destination as the Type and Click on Continue.

6. On the next page, you need to enter the URL of your thank you page. This is the page that someone who fills the form will get to see. You need a form and a thank you page to track goal conversions.

7. You can even enter a monetary value for the goal through the Value toggle button. You can skip this option initially if there is no monetary value attached to the goal. You can skip the Funnel option as well.

8. Then click on Save.

9. Now the Goal has been set up. You will now get data for the conversion goal. You will get information on the page from which contributed to the action of the form being filled and how many times the form is filled.

Creating a Dashboard

1. Click on Customization and then click Dashboards on your Google Analytics home screen.

2. Click on Create for new Dashboards.

3. You can select a Blank or Starter Dashboard. Then provide your Dashboard a name. As you click on Create Dashboard, you will be navigated to your dashboard.

4. Choosing a Starter Dashboard will give you certain default widgets. You can also add more widgets through the Add Widget button on the top left corner of your dashboard.

5. As you click on Add Widget, you need to provide the Widget title. You can select the visualization of your data as a number, a timeline, a map, a table, a pie chart, or a bar graph.

6. You can select the visualization for Standard data or Real-time data (live). You should choose Standard as a beginner.

7. You can then add a metric; you want to see on the dashboard. You can add different kinds of filters to get the data you want to monitor.

8. As you click on Save, your widget will be available on the dashboard. You can customize the widgets from the dashboard.

9. You can create a Private or Shared dashboard. The Private dashboard will be only visible to you. Shared dashboards can be used by your teammates. Any changes your teammates make in their shared dashboard will not be visible to you.

Dashboards are a great way to easily access the data that you would like to monitor on a regular basis.

Reports

There are five main reports in Google Analytics that provide detailed information on your website performance and on your visitors.

1. Realtime
2. Audiences
3. Acquisition
4. Behavior
5. Conversions

1. **Realtime**

The real-time reports give insights into real-time information about your website. It gives you information on the website visitors that are presently active.

This report may sound exciting but is not of much value. It is only useful if you have run a marketing campaign on a certain day, and you want to track how effective is the campaign in real time. For example, you can track how many people are active on your website during a flash sale.

2. **Audience**

The Audience tab on the left menu is the most important section of your Google Analytics account. It gives information on which country your website visitors are from, what languages they speak, and how they access your site (browser and OS). You can also get data on the demographics of your users, such as the age and gender of your website visitors. It can even give you some information about their interests.

As you click on Active users, this tab will show you how many users had at least one session on your website in the past day, past seven days, or past 30 days. The higher the number of active users on your website, the better it is. It also shows how engaging your website is for the users.

The Interests reports show you the preferences of your website visitors. It will help you know your target audiences much better, and it also will let you know whether your site is reaching the right people or not. It will also help you to drive your content strategy. You will know which topics you should cover in your blogs more as per the interest level of your target audiences.

In the Demographics tab under Audience, you will find the age and gender of your target audience. This information is beneficial to know whether you are targeting the right audience. For example, if your website is selling designer bags to females, then your demographic data should show a higher percentage of female website visitors.

In the Geo tab under Audiences, you will find two tabs Language and Location. In the Location tab, you find the City, Continent, or Subcontinent. You can view the New Users column in the Location report to know which countries or cities you are getting your new users from. This will help you identify new markets.

You can find out which country is giving you more goal conversions and even the cities from where you are getting more conversions. You can use the right keywords to increase traffic from particular cities.

The language tab in the Audience Geo tab lets you know the language of your website visitors.

If you are getting more traffic from a place where people speak a different language than the language on your website, your site will have a high bounce rate.

3. **Behavior**

In the Behaviour tab, you will find information about your website visitors. You can find out how many new visitors are there on your website as compared to the visitors who are returning to your website in the New Vs. Returning tab. You can use this report to see whether you have a good percentage of returning visitors, which means higher engagement and loyalty of the visitors.

The Technology reports in the Behavior tab will let you know which browsers and devices your website visitors are using. For example, if you are getting a lot of mobile users with a high bounce rate, you need to optimize your website for mobile browsers. The mobile website design should be as such that it is easier for visitors to find the right information, and it should be easy to complete the conversion goals.

4. **Acquisition**

Acquisition reports (Figure 6.2) will be very helpful in creating and editing your content to get more website visitors and engage them. It will help you make data-backed decisions.

Google Analytics helps you track the source/medium from which the website visitors came.

The Medium is categorized into:

Organic: This medium indicates that someone landed on your website using a search query in the search engine such as Google. Organic users land on your site by getting your website URLs in the Google search results.

CPC: The website visitors that landed on your website by clicking on any of the paid ads that you are running through Google Ads. The ads can be search ads that appear in Google search results or display ads that are run on a different website.

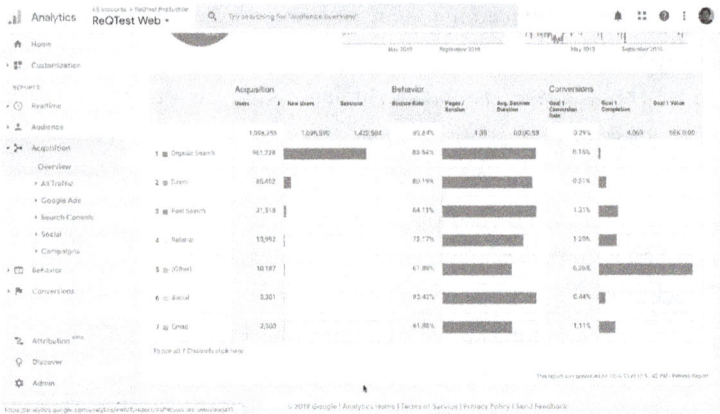

Figure 6.2 Acquisition

Google and the Google logo are registered trademarks of Google LLC, used with permission.

Referrals: The referral medium comprises those website visitors who land on your website through your website links on some other website.

E-mail: The e-mail medium comprises of website visitors that came on your website through an e-mail marketing campaign.

None: This comprises users who directly came to your website by typing your website URL in their browsers. The source of these users is direct, and their medium is none.

Source: This provides more specific information about the medium. For example, if the medium is a referral for some website visitor, then the source will provide the exact URL from which your user came. If the medium of a website visitor is organic, then the source would be the name of the search engine it came from, such as Google, Bing, Yahoo, and so on.

You can view any of your reports as per the time period for which you want to see the data. You can select the exact dates between which you want to see the data. You can even compare the data with some other time period. For example, you can compare the data of August month with that of July month for a particular year.

You can use the Source/Medium report to know which is the channel that gives you the most website visitors. You can also get to know the quality of the visitors from a particular channel. A lower bounce rate indicates the quality of the website visitor is good.

Channels: The channels report gives you the traffic by channels such as Organic search, social, direct, and so on. This is very helpful to get the performance report on how your blogs are doing in the search engines. You can click on the Organic search in the Channels data table. Click on the Landing Page button above the table. You will get the URL of the blogs along with the number of visitors on a particular blog, its bounce rate, and the number of goal conversion.

This is one of the most critical matrices you will be using for your content marketing strategy more often. You can find your top-performing blogs based on conversion goals and the number of visitors. You can choose to pick the topics that are getting you more conversions and website visitors.

5. **Conversion**

   You create a website for a purpose. Let us suppose an interior designer Natalia has created a website to schedule a home visit for a consultation. There is a page on her website with a form to "Book a consultation." She has set up a goal in Google Analytics to track how many people provide their details through this form. Every time on this form submission, a conversion happens.

In Google Analytics, a conversion is the completion of an activity that is crucial for your business. A conversion could be signing up as a blog subscriber, making a purchase, booking a demo, opting for a free trial, and so on. The conversion tab in Google Analytics gives you insight into the performance of your website in terms of the completion of the goals. Ideally, you should not have more than two to three goals to track your marketing performance.

For an e-commerce website, you need to set up a tracking code. The e-commerce platforms such as Shopify, WooCommerce, Magento, and so on, provide their analytics for monitoring the website performance. For your e-commerce website, it's better to use the analytics of your website platform.

This report gives you information on the conversion of your website. It provides the goal conversion rate, the total number of goals completed, goal value and the total abandonment rate of goals.

Tracking Marketing Campaign

You may be running different marketing campaigns on various channels. For example, you are running a blogging campaign on highly relevant keywords with high search volume on your website. You may be running an e-mail campaign to convert your blog subscribers into leads. You may be running a social media campaign to drive engagement. You can track all these campaigns all together through campaign tracking. For campaign tracking, you need to add a campaign tag to identify the source of the users.

There are five campaign tags to any URL to identify the source of your campaign traffic:

Medium

This tells how your message reached the users; the medium could be e-mail, CPC (paid search), or social media networks.

Source

This tag helps to identify the source of the traffic. For example, the medium is e-mail; then the source will help you determine which e-mail campaign the user came from.

Campaign

This helps to identify the campaign from which the visitors came from. This is very useful when you are running multiple campaigns. You can quickly identify the specific marketing campaign with which the user interacted with and came to your website.

Content

This tag helps you do A/B testing of your content. For example, you have sent out two versions of e-mail, and you want to know which version is more effective. You can use the content tag to differentiate the two versions of the e-mail.

Term

This tag is used for paid search campaigns to identify the keywords. This is used when you want to tag paid search campaigns manually.

Creating these URLs is rather easy as Google provides a URL builder. You can search for the Google URL builder in the search engine. It will land you on the page that automatically creates a URL for campaign tracking.

URL Builder

Here are the fields on URL builder:

Website URL

You need to provide the URL of the landing page you want to track. For example, you are running a Google paid search campaign, and you have created a landing page. You can provide the URL of the landing page to track the page visitors.

Campaign Source

You can provide the source of the campaign. In the above example, you can give value as Google.

Campaign Medium

As the medium of the campaign is paid, you can provide CPC as the value.

Campaign Term

You can provide the search term you want to track that visitors are using to land on your page. This is an optional field.

Campaign Content

This is an optional field that you can use for A/B testing of your content, as described above.

Campaign Name

You can keep the name as such that it easy for you to identify in Google Analytics.

It is better to use single words for the tags, but if you use multiple words, then the URL builder will add underscore between the words. The tags are case sensitive, a campaign tag such as "discounts" will be different from "DISCOUNTS."

A URL will be generated for tracking website visitors. You can test the URL that you have just created by opening in an incognito window (private window) of your browser. You can click on some links in the e-mail that you want to track. You can see the data in your Google Analytics in real-time reports or standard reports.

Just click on Acquisition Campaigns All Campaigns, you can search the marketing campaign you want to track. You can open the campaign and see the conversion data.

You can track different campaigns using the same mechanism in Google Analytics. This will help you identify which of your campaigns are most effective in bringing about the results that you want to accomplish.

Important Metrics

Some important metrics to know:

Average Time on Page

This metrics is calculated based on the time a visitor spends on a page before moving on to a new page of the website. The average time is calculated on the total time spent on different pages divided by the number of pages visited.

Pages/ Session

This metrics helps to identify how many unique pages visitors view during their session.

Average Session Duration

It is the average time spent by the user on the website.

Bounce Rate

This metrics helps to identify the percentage of users who have visited just a single page on your website and left.

Points to Remember

1. Google Analytics will let you know how people are landing on your website.

   It will let you know what people are doing on your website.

2. You will be able to learn which page of your website is getting the most traffic (visitors).

3. Google Analytics account is structured into
   - Organization
   - Account
   - Property
   - View

4. There are five main reports in Google Analytics
   1. Realtime reports
   2. Audience reports
   3. Behavior reports
   4. Acquisition
   5. Conversions

5. Realtime reports gives you information on the website visitors that are active on the website at present.

6. Audience reports gives information on which country your website visitors are in, what languages they speak, and how they access your site (browser and OS) their interests, and so on.

7. Behavior reports gives information such as how many new visitors as compared to the visitors who are returning to your website in the New Vs. Returning tab. The Technology reports in the Behavior tab will let you know which browsers and devices your website visitors are using.

8. Acquisition reports will be very helpful in tweaking your content and marketing strategy. It will help you make data-backed decisions.

9. You can track all these campaigns all together through campaign tracking.

Assignment

1. Set up a Google Analytics account for your website.
2. Visit all the five different reports and note down three insights you gain from each report.
3. Create a campaign tracking URL using the URL builder and track the campaign results.

CHAPTER 7

Search Engine Marketing

Search engine marketing was earlier a term that included both Search Engine Optimization (SEO) and Paid Search. Now Search Engine Marketing is mainly used for Paid Search campaigns.

In simpler terms, Search Engine Marketing is the process of gaining visibility of your products or services in the search engine results pages by running paid search ads or Pay-Per-Click (PPC) campaigns. The benefit of running a paid campaign is that you will be targeting the audience who are already motivated to buy.

SEM Versus SEO

Search Engine Marketing refers to running paid search advertisements by paying to the search engine, whereas Search Engine Optimization is done without paying anything to the search engine.

You might be curious if you can make your website visible in the search results by free SEO, then why should you be spending money on paid campaigns. The answer to this lies in understanding the difference between SEO and SEM.

SEO is a slow process, and it takes time for a website to rank on specific keywords. The blogs written for SEO purposes are mainly written to drive relevant traffic to your site. A lot of on-page and off-page efforts are required for SEO, and there is still no guarantee that your website pages will be visible in the top search results.

SEM, on the other hand, gives you instant results. Through paid ads, you will target the audiences who are about to make a purchase decision.

Let's take an example; you have recently created a website that sells perfumes. You have started with your SEO strategy to write keyword-oriented search engine optimized blogs. You have so far written four blogs on your website. You search for a specific keyword in Google to find your oldest blog, and it is still stuck on the third page of Google search results. You find that all the results on the first page of Google for your selected keywords are from well-established brands that have been in the industry for decades.

For a new website to rank organically, it will take time and effort for the on-page and off-page efforts to kick in.

In this case, you can run Google Ad campaigns to target people who are looking to buy perfumes. You may be losing out to your competitors organically, but you can outperform your competitors through paid search campaigns.

A combination of SEO and SEM is the most effective digital marketing strategy for your business.

How Does Paid Search Work?

Whenever a user types specific keywords on which you are running your paid ads in the search engine, your ad copies will appear in the search results. Getting your ad copies in the search results for specific keywords depends on how effectively you have structured your paid search campaigns and how well you are running them.

There a combination of different factors that makes your ad appear on a specific spot on the Search Engine Result Page (SERP). The overall goal of Pay-Per-Click advertising is to get people to your website or landing pages and make them take a specific action.

The spot at which your ad appears on a search engine result page is decided based on bidding that takes place for a keyword.

Many businesses would want to be shown on the first page of the search results. There are a limited number of ad spots available for a keyword, and there are auctions that decide the ad spot.

The search engines provide platforms such as Google Ads and Bing Ads to advertisers to bid for keywords to run their ads. The advertisers pay when people engage with the advertisements that are measured through impressions (views) or clicks.

Google Ads

Google Ads is the paid advertising platform that lets you run paid campaigns on the Pay-Per-Click and Cost-Per-Impressions basis using Google search engine and Google's network of sites.

Google is, without a doubt, the most popular search engine across the globe. There are 3.5 billion search queries entered into Google each day. There are other search engines Bing and Yahoo, but Google dominates the search engine market with over 72 percent of users.

Google Ads will provide you a platform with a high return on investment. Advertisers make on an average $2 for every $1 they invest according to Google's Economic Impact Report.

Google provides a variety of options to run your ads on Google's different products. You can run your campaigns on:

- You-Tube
- Gmail
- Google Maps
- Google search results
- Partner websites
- Mobile app downloads

Re-marketing ads are a great way to engage your website visitors who didn't purchase from your business initially.

Why Should You Advertise on Google Ads?

As discussed earlier, your SEO efforts will take some time to kick in. Getting your website pages on the top Google search results will take a lot of time and patience for your chosen keywords.

Writing 2,000 words for a highly research-oriented article will take at least 6 hours. For your blog to rank in the top 10 search results will need some backlinks from some high authority sites depending on the keyword difficulty. Similarly, with your social media strategy, you will require a lot of time and effort to increase the engagement on your social media pages.

With Google Ads, you will be generating leads and sales within min-utes of your launching your Google Ads campaign.

The blogs you write for the purposes of SEO help you target audi-ences that are in the initial phase of their buyer journey. For example, if you are into a business of selling smart TV, you would write a blog on "smart TV buying guide" to make your target audience aware of your brand online. This way, you will target an audience who has just started with researching smart TVs, and they intend to get well informed before making a purchase decision.

While if someone uses the search term "55 inches smart TV," their search intent is to buy a smart TV online. You would want to show your Google Ad to someone with this search intent.

With Google Ads, you choose the keywords that will drive sales for your business.

Elements of a Google Ads Account

- Ad Campaign
- Ad Groups
- Keywords
- Ad text
- Landing pages

Let's understand the Google Ads account set up with an example. Your real-estate business offers three different services, such as Renting, Purchasing, and Leasing properties. You want to run paid search cam-paigns for all these services.

You can set up your Google Ads account with three Ad Campaigns for Renting Properties, Purchasing Properties, and Leasing Properties. In the Renting Properties Ad Campaign, you can create two different Ad Groups for Renting Apartment and Renting Office Space. In the Renting Apartment Ad Groups, you can keep all the keywords related to renting an apartment.

You can then add Ad Copies and Landing Pages for the keywords. You can even segregate Ad Campaigns based on locations, seasonal discounts, and so on. You must structure your Google Ads account in a way it's easier to implement campaign level changes.

So your Google Ads account has Ad Campaigns at the highest level. In the Ad Campaign, you have different ad groups. Each Ad group consists of keywords and ad copies.

Google Ad Campaigns

Google network provides you to run three types of Ad Campaigns.

Search Ads

The search ads are the text ads that appear in the Google search results. You may have noticed ads appear in your Google search results when you search for a product.

Display Ads

The display ads are the image-based ads that are shown on the web pages in Google Display Network.

Video Ads

You would find these ads in your YouTube videos.

We will be discussing the most commonly used Search ads and Display ads. As a beginner, you should master search ads as it gives you working knowledge of Google Ads.

Running Your Google Ads

Set Up Google Ads Account

You can create a Google Ads account for free; you can search for Google Ads in the search engine and navigate to ads.google.com. You just need to provide your e-mail and website URL to get started. Setting up a Google Ads account is an intuitive process.

While setting up the account, Google Ads interface will ask you to set up your first Ad campaign in which you need to set up budgets, targeting, bidding, and writing your first text ad.

Initially, you should start with a small daily budget. You should first run your campaigns to get a working knowledge of Google Ads before investing more money. You can choose the locations of your target audience.

You will get a lot of insights into your industry as well as how users are engaging with your ads once you start running your campaign.

Select Search Network and Display Network

Initially, you would be using the Search Network to run search ads, and later for re-marketing purposes, you can use display ads. I would suggest always start with search ads, and once you are well versed with Google Ads, you can go for display advertising. At times, display advertising can exhaust your budget pretty fast, and your ads will get displayed on unrelated sites if you have not correctly set your display campaigns.

Initially, you should let Google bid automatically. You can set the bids manually once you get reports on how much a click costs.

Write the first ad copy that you think will motivate people to click on your ad. You can take the help of a copywriter to write best converting ad copies.

As a practice, you should try to find out which ads are running in Google search results on the keyword you are targeting. You will get to learn which ad is on the top and what does the ad copy say and when you click on the ad copy, what is written on the landing page.

If no ads are running on your keywords, then you will not get ads in Google search results. Try different keywords to get some relevant advertisements in the search results that you can analyze. You will use Google's Keyword Planner tool available in the Google Ads platform to find out the keywords you should run your ads on.

You need to ensure the Google Analytics account of your website is linked with your Google Ads account. Navigate to the Admin tab of your Google Analytics account. You will find the Product Linking option with Google Ads Linking option to connect your Google Ads account with Google Analytics.

You should also use the Urchin Tracking Module (UTM) codes to track your Google Ads Landing Pages. UTM codes are used to create a custom URL for tracking campaigns. You can use the Campaign builder, as mentioned in the chapter on Google Analytics, to monitor the keywords, the ad group, the landing page that got the conversion.

Steps to Start Running Google Ads Campaigns

1. Do keyword research
2. Set up the Ad campaign
3. Set up the Ad group
4. Write the Ad copies
5. Add your landing pages
6. Add negative keywords

Keyword Research: Finding the Keywords to Run the Ads On

As you create your Google Ads account, the next step would be to research the keywords that your target audiences use. In the Google Ads interface, click on Tools and Settings tab. Click on Keyword Planner in the first column, "Planning."

You start with keywords that identify your product or services. For example, if you are selling chocolates, then you can use this keyword to search for relevant keywords. The Keyword Planner will give you average monthly searches for a keyword and competition.

Average monthly searches are the average number of times people have searched for the exact keyword in a month.

The competition defines the number of ads that are running on that keyword. The higher the competition, the higher would be the bid for getting your ad on top. You should go for less competitive keywords.

Long-Tail Keywords

The long-tail keywords have a longer search phrase with more specific keywords to search for anything. For example, "Buy leather jackets online cheap," "best long lasting perfumes for men," or "best adventure treks in California."

Although these specific search phrases will have a lower search volume and lower competition, the chances of conversion would be higher. You can use the Keyword Planner by typing in a long-tail keyword, which will help someone find your business online.

Create a list of keywords and segregate them based on relevance. For example, if you have found 20 keywords and out of those 10 keywords are related to product 1, and the other ten keywords are related to product 2, you can segregate the keywords based on products in your list.

Setting Up the Ad Campaign

As you have a list of keywords, you can start setting up Ad Campaign. On the home page of your Google Ads, click on "Campaigns." You will be navigated to a page where you will find a blue + sign on the screen on the left-hand side. Click on it and then click on +New campaign (Figure 7.1).

On the next page, you will be asked to select a goal; you can choose the last option "Create a campaign without goal's guidance." You can then select the campaign type as Search. Skip the results you want to get for now and click on Continue.

You can then type in the name of your campaign. If you are doing segmentation based on product/service/offering in your campaign, then name the campaign accordingly. If you are doing the product—and location-wise campaign segmentation, then you should name your campaign,

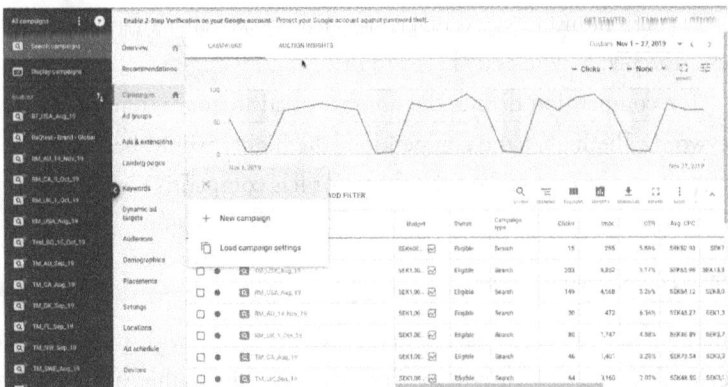

Figure 7.1 Setting up the Ad campaign

Google and the Google logo are registered trademarks of Google LLC, used with permission.

including the product and location—for example, Perfumes_US, perfumes_Canada, and so on.

The idea behind naming your campaign is that you should be able to identify the purpose of the ad campaign and which ad groups, keywords, ad copies, and landing page you will associate with the campaign.

Select the network as a "Search Network." There is a "Show More" settings option in the next row. Click on it to set the start date and end date of running your ad. Initially, you should run your ad for one or two weeks to analyze how well are you doing with your ad campaigns. This will also control your budget spend. If you are running your ad indefinitely, Google will keep running the ad campaign and exhausting your budget.

The location tab is important if you want to reach a specific area to run your ad. You can run your ads in the locations based on zip codes as well. This is very relevant when the customer in the vicinity of your physical location will purchase your product or service. For example, for a gym in Los Angeles, it would be more fruitful to run Google Ads for people in the vicinity of the gym rather than showing their ads to someone in Florida. Skip the Language settings option. Google Ads will suggest the language.

Audience setting is used when you are running a display campaign. For the search campaign, you can skip this option as well.

You can set your daily budget and keep the Delivery method as standard initially. The accelerated method will spend your budget fast.

In the Bidding option, select "Clicks" in what do you want to focus on. Initially, you are not aware of what your conversion rate is, and you have no data, so you should start with clicks.

You can set a maximum cost per click bid limit. For example, if your daily budget is $10, then you can set a maximum cost per click as $2. For different keywords, the cost per click is different; you may be shelling out even $30. You will get more insights as you run your campaign from your data. You can also get the bidding price for a particular keyword in Keyword Planner.

In the next row, where you have "Show More" settings option, you can set the Ad schedule through this option. This setting is very important if you want to run your ads on specific days during a specific time.

For example, a consulting business would want to run its ads on business days that is, is Mondays–Fridays and stop running their ads on weekends. Similarly, for an e-commerce site, weekends might be more suitable for running their ads as compared to weekdays.

As you set your Ad schedule, you can click on "Save and Continue."

Skip the Ad extensions initially. You can always edit your campaign and change your settings. The Ad extensions help you drive more clicks on your ads. If you are getting a lot of impressions (views in search results) on your ads, but very few people are clicking on your ad, then you can try using different extensions to boost click through rate of your ads. Here are some common ad extensions.

Sitelink Extensions

The site links provide additional links to your sites in the ad copy that appears in Google Search results. It gives more exciting information to make people click on them.

Callout Extensions

These extensions help you provide additional information about your product or service. A callout extension is 25 characters long and is used to communicate a feature or benefit in a Google ad.

Call Extensions

This extension is used to add your phone number in your Google ad. You can use your sales number or your customer service team number to allow anyone to reach out to you directly.

There are other extensions that you can choose to include in your ad. Always keep in mind that the purpose of ad extension is to get more clicks on your ad from your target audience. Include ad extensions that facilitate this purpose.

Setting Up Ad groups

Now you will be asked to name your Ad Groups and Add keywords in them. Based on the keyword list that you have, you can start adding keywords. You should create different Ad groups based on different keywords. The keywords you add to your ad groups can have different keyword match types.

Keywords Match Types

Keyword match types allow you to set when your ad is triggered based on the keywords. The match type you are using will help you reach out to your target audience.

Broad Match

The default match type is a broad match that is assigned to all the keywords you run your ads on. Broad match will let you reach the widest audiences as it will trigger your ads when any of your broad match keywords appear in the user's search query in any order.

The broad match includes not only the keyword you choose but its synonyms, misspellings, related searches, and relevant variations. For example, if your keyword is "men's perfume," then your ad would be triggered for "men's fragrance" and as well as "men's cologne." Your ad will also be triggered by the "men's wallet."

The broad match type will help your ad to be visible to a maximum number of people, and the downside of using broad match type is that your ad will be triggered on irrelevant searches. The clicks from the audience that are not looking to buy your product will cost you deductions of your Ad word budget.

Broad Match Modifier

It is an advanced version of the broad match where you can control when your ad appears in the search results. You can add a "+" in front of any keyword to use broad match modifier when you place + in front of a keyword, your ad only appears when the user search query has your keyword.

For example, in the above example, where we used men's perfume, if you use your keywords like men's +perfume, your ad will only be triggered when the user search query includes the keyword perfume. The search queries could be "expensive perfume," "car perfume," and so on. If you set both keywords using + sign +men's + perfume, your ad will appear only when both the keywords are there in the search query. The search queries could be "best men's perfume," "cheap men's perfume," men's perfume under 500, How to select a perfume for men, and so on.

The ad will appear when both the keywords are present in the search query. They can be in any order.

Phrase Match

The Phrase Match offers greater control over when your ad will appear in the search results. Setting the keywords as a phrase match will make your ad appear only when your keywords appear in the exact order in the search query. There might be other words before or after the phrase match keywords you have set. Keeping your keywords inside the quotations marks designates the phrase match.

For example, if you set the phrase match of keywords "rent apartment," your ad will appear when the user searches for "rent apartment in the city center," "a website to rent an apartment, and so on." The ad would not appear for searches such as rent flat, rent luxury apartment, and so on.

Exact Match

This match type will make your ad appear only when the user searches the exact term or close variations. To set keywords as an exact match, you keep the keywords inside brackets [keywords]. Earlier, Google Ads only appear when the user typed in the exact term for the exact match keywords, but this way, a lot of the times, the ad would not appear when the user had used the close variation of the keyword with the same search intent.

Exact match helps you to reduce the irrelevant clicks you get on your ad, but on the other hand, it also limits the traffic on your ads.

For example, if you set the exact match of keywords "smartwatch for men," your ad will appear when the user searches for "smartwatch for men."

Writing Ad Copies

As you are done with finding out the keywords, the next step would be to create ad copies for each ad group. Your ad copy should include the keyword in the ad group.

Ad Headline

Your ad headline is limited to 25 characters to grab your target audience. Your Ad headline will help you get clicks on your ad. The new Dynamic Keyword Insertion allows Google to automatically insert exact keywords of your ad group into your ad copy (Figure 7.2).

Below your ad headline, there would be your ad copy with two lines that have 35 characters each. You may feel that 35 characters won't be enough to describe your offering. You can define the benefits of your business, or you can describe the features. You should always ensure that your ad headline and ad copy makes it clear to the audience what you offer. If your ad copy is confusing or doesn't give clear information about what you offer, then you will be wasting money on clicks without getting conversions.

Add Your Landing Pages

For every ad copy, you will have a landing page on which someone who clicks the ad will land. The sole purpose of your landing page is conversion.

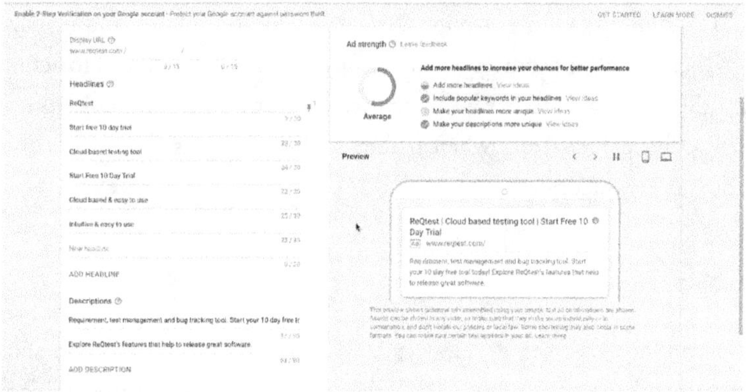

Figure 7.2 Ad headline

Google and the Google logo are registered trademarks of Google LLC, used with permission.

A person types in a query to search for a product or service, your ad is triggered as your ad copy contains the keywords. Your ad appears in the search results; the person finds your ad copy exciting and clicks on the advertisement. The person is then navigated to your landing page.

The landing page is where the conversion will happen. Landing pages are usually individual pages on your website, which are created for a user to take a specific action. The action could be to purchase a product, sign up for a free trial, or take any action that generates sales or leads for your business.

The landing page doesn't have a menu like the other pages of your website. There is no navigation to any external page as the only purpose for the user is to take a specific action.

You may find businesses using their home page or feature pages as their landing pages. This is a bad practice if you are looking to generate revenue from your Google Ads investment. Using your website home page or any other page can be a good strategy for brand awareness but not good for generating leads or sales.

The best practice is that each of your ad groups should have keywords that you also use on your landing page.

The landing page content should convey the same message as your ad copy. For example, if your ad copy headline says, "Dark Chocolate cakes," and on your landing page, you have mentioned all types of cakes you offer. The person who clicked on your ad was exactly looking to buy a dark chocolate cake. If he doesn't find a dark chocolate cake in the first fold of your landing page, the person will navigate away from your landing page.

There are also instances when ad copy shows a different call to action, and the landing page has a different call to action. For example, the ad copy offers a Free Trial, whereas the landing page has the main call to action as Contact sales.

Value Proposition

Your landing page should have your value proposition, which is a short statement that explains the value of the product to your potential customers. The value proposition and your lead capturing form should be on the first fold of the landing page.

Add Negative Keywords

The keyword match type is already discussed above. You also need to add some negative keywords. These keywords will let Google know on which keywords you don't want your ads to run.

As you run your ads campaign, you will find that a lot of times your ads are triggered on keywords that are no way relevant to your business. You can add these keywords as negative keywords. The negative keywords are really helpful in ensuring your ads are triggered for relevant keywords, especially when you use Phrase Match and Broad Match type. In the Exact match type, your ads are triggered only for relevant keywords.

The negative keywords are the keywords on which you don't want your ads to be triggered. For example, if you are into the business of men's perfume, you don't want your ad to be triggered on men's shoes. You can set "shoes" as a negative keyword. You will also see a lot of user's search keywords when you run your ad campaigns. You can mark the keywords that are not relevant to your brand as negative keywords.

Negative keywords can also be of three types:

- Negative Broad Match
- Negative Phrase Match
- Negative Exact Match

The negative keyword matches work exactly as the broad match, phrase match, and exact match; it is just your ads will not appear on the keywords you set as negative keywords.

To add negative keywords, click on "Keywords," and then you will find the second tab as "Negative Keywords." Add some negative keywords in the, and you can choose a campaign for which you have added a negative keyword (Figure 7.3).

The other approach will be to go to a specific campaign and then click on Keywords on the left-hand pane. Click on the "Search Terms" tab. This tab shows the keywords that were used by the people who clicked on your ad copy. You can mark the term that is not relevant as negative keywords.

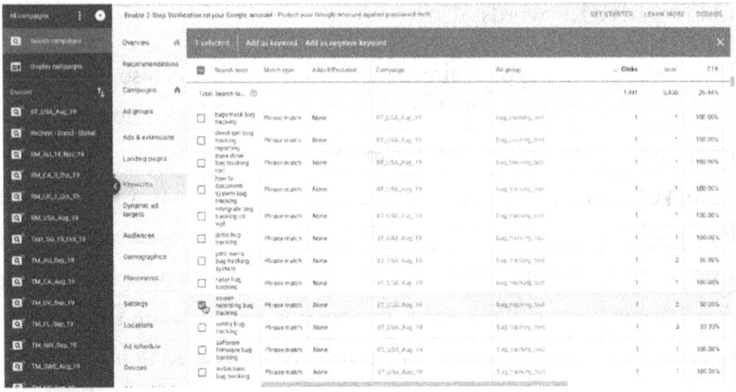

Figure 7.3 Add negative keywords

Google and the Google logo are registered trademarks of Google LLC, used with permission.

Most of the steps are similar in running basic display campaigns. I would suggest that you should first run Google Search campaigns, monitor the results you are getting in Google Ads regularly. As a beginner, you should focus only on your search campaigns, and as you gain confidence, you can start with display campaigns.

Make the changes in your Google Ads based on your findings, such as how many impressions, clicks, and conversions you are getting. What is the cost that you are spending per click and per conversion? How many leads are you generating through your Google Ad? How can you improve the efficiency of your Google Ads campaign?

You should also be aware of some crucial terms in Google Ads:

AdRank

Your AdRank will determine where your ad will be visible in the search results paid ads section. A higher AdRank implicates a better placement of your ad that will help to get more visibility and clicks on your ad. Your AdRank is your maximum bid multiplied by your Quality Score.

Ad Rank = Maximum bid × Quality Score.

Quality Score

The Quality Score is a way to measure the quality of your ad depending on the click through rate (CTR), the relevance of the keywords, the quality of the landing page, and past performance in the search results.

Bidding

Google Ads provides you a bidding mechanism where you can select the maximum bid amount you are ready to pay for a single click on your ad. The higher the bid amount, the better would be the placement.

The bidding options for Google Ads are as follows:

- Cost Per Click (CPC): The amount you will pay for each click on your ad.
- Cost Per Mile (CPM): The amount you will have to pay for one thousand ad impressions, which means when your ad is shown to a thousand people.
- Cost Per Engagement (CPM): This is the amount that you will have to pay when someone takes a predefined action on your ad.

Click-Through Rate (CTR)

The Click-Through Rate helps you to know the percentage of the clicks you got on your ads compared to the number of views of your ad. The higher the CTR, means higher is the relevancy of your ad copies and the keywords on which you are running your ads.

Conversion Rate

The conversion rate helps you to know the number of form submissions compared to the total number of visitors on your website. Let's say 100 visitors reach the landing page by clicking on your ad. Out of these 100 visitors, 20 visitors filled the lead generation form. The conversion rate would be 20 percent. A higher conversion rate means that the overall landing page experience is excellent, which is driving conversions.

Monitor Your Google Ads

You should be evaluating each for the following metrics:

Cost Per Conversion

The cost per conversion is the cost spent per conversion.

Ad Spend/Conversions = Cost per conversion

For example, if you have been running four different campaigns and your conversion goal is to get sign-up for a form. You have run your campaigns for a week, and the total cost spent on your ads is $200. You have got 20 form signs ups through your search ads.

In this case, your cost per conversion would be

200/20 = 10

So you are spending $10 per conversion.

The conversion goal for the different industries would be different, and so would be the cost per conversion. For an industry, a cost per conversion of $200 may be very high, and for another industry, it may be reasonable.

You can know through your cost per conversion which campaigns are performing well and which campaigns are underperforming.

You can choose to reallocate the budget of your underperforming campaigns to your performing campaigns. You may choose to scale the performing campaigns and tweak your other campaigns based on the observation of your performing campaigns.

Conversion Rate

It helps to measure the conversion concerning clicks the ad received.

Conversions/ Clicks on the ad × 100 = Conversion rate

The conversion rate will help you to analyze your landing page effectiveness. A higher conversion rate means a better landing page message and experience.

Getting more clicks and fewer conversions mean a lower conversion rate, and then you should:

1. Add/replace your Call to Action (CTA) on the landing page.
2. Change your Landing Page Content to improve the message you are communicating.
3. Change the design of your landing page to engage visitors visually.

If you have a higher conversion rate, then you can use a similar landing page for other ad campaigns, as well.

Search Impression Share

You can find these metrics in the Columns Modify Columns Competitive metrics tab. Your ad would be running based on your specific keywords. It is not 100 percent of the time that your ad will be visible to your target audience.

If the Search Impression Share for a campaign is 75 percent, then it means if there are 100 opportunities for your ad to be shown. It shows 75 times out of the 100 opportunities.

To improve your search impression share, you need to change your budget allocation and Quality Score.

Quality Score is a very critical factor for your ad campaigns. You should always focus on improving the Quality Score of your keywords. You should check your ad copy to improve its click-through rate that impacts the Quality Score.

Initially, while running your ad campaigns, you will have a lower search impression share, so you should look at this data after running your Google Ad campaign for at least two months.

Apart from tracking these campaign metrics, you should also monitor the quality of the leads that you are getting if your conversion goal is not sales. For an e-commerce company that is selling a product, it is easier to find out the effectiveness of their Google Ads through the revenue they are generating. For a service company, if their conversion goal is to book a consultation, then they need to evaluate whether the leads that are coming in through Google Ads are converting into sales or not.

Points to Remember

1. Search Engine Marketing is the process to get visibility of your products or services in the search engine results pages by running Paid Search ads or Pay-Per-Click (PPC) campaigns.
2. Google Ads is the paid advertising platform that lets you run paid campaigns on the Pay-Per-Click and Cost-Per-Impressions basis using Google search engine and Google's network of sites.
3. Getting your website pages on the top Google Search results will take a lot of time and patience for your chosen keywords.

4. With Google Ads, you will be generating leads and sales within minutes of your launching your Google Ads campaign.

5. Elements of a Google Ads account:
   - Ad Campaign
   - Ad Groups
   - Keywords
   - Ad text
   - Landing pages

6. Steps to start running Google Ads:
   1. Do keyword research
   2. Set up the Ad campaign
   3. Set up the Ad group
   4. Write the Ad copies
   5. Add your landing pages
   6. Add negative keywords

7. Keywords Match Types
   Keyword match types allow you to set when your ad is triggered based on the keywords.
   - Broad Match
   - Broad Match Modifier
   - Phrase Match
   - Exact Match

Assignment

1. Set up your Google Ad Account and use the Keyword Planner tool to find out 20 relevant keywords to your product or services.

2. Create two different campaigns and create Ad groups to segregate your chosen keywords logically.

3. Create ad copies for your ad groups and create one landing page each for your ad groups.

4. Run your ad campaign on automatic bidding mode for two weeks.

5. Analyze the different metrics outlined in this chapter after running your ads for two weeks.

6. List down all the action steps you need to take in Google Ads to improve the number of clicks and conversion based on your analysis.

CHAPTER 8

Online Reputation Management

As you establish and execute your digital marketing strategy, your brand would start gaining more visibility over the Internet.

People will be engaging with your brand and talking about your brand. They may be expressing opinions about your brand through blog posts comments, social media posts, or writing your product or service reviews on various forums.

The Internet has given a voice to your customers to express their opinions. Not all of their views would be positive. These user-generated content can make or break your brand's reputation online.

What Is Online Reputation Management (ORM)?

Online reputation management (ORM) is the process of monitoring and addressing mentions of your brand over the Internet in a bid to build a positive online image. ORM also includes maintaining good personal relations with influencers and users to get positive user-generated content for your brand.

The end goal of ORM is to create a positive public perception of an individual, organization, or brand entity over the Internet. ORM helps to mitigate the effects of any negative image.

Let's understand this with an example. You run an e-commerce portal online that offers organic products. One of your shipments reached the customer 10 days later than the scheduled delivery date. To add to the frustrations of the customer, the product delivered was not of good quality.

The customer got agitated and used all the possible Internet channels to vent out his anger. He wrote negative reviews about your delivery and product quality on Google Reviews. He tweeted negative things about your brand and posted a negative review on your Facebook channel.

Now, whenever someone searches your brand and products online, the first thing that comes up in Google search results, Facebook search, and other social media platforms search results are the negative reviews that the customers posted. As the people read all the bad reviews about your brand, they will rethink their decision to purchase from your brand. A customer venting out on different social channels may sound like an aggravated situation, but even well established brands have to face customer fury at some point in time.

Even the employers before hiring someone search on Google and social media networks to find anything negative about a candidate. The employers try to find out what you are posting about yourself on social networks or what others are saying about you if they intend to hire you.

The possible impacts of a bad reputation online are:

- Lost credibility and trust in your brand
- Drop in sales
- Increase in the numbers of customers churning
- Drop in the share prices
- Discord in investor relationship and partnership breakdown
- Increase in employee attrition
- Your brand equity is harmed

These are just some negative impacts of a bad reputation.

What Could Lead to a Negative Brand Perception?

The negative brand perception is built over time, similar to the time it takes time to create a positive impression.

No Social Media Presence

At times businesses tend to ignore the importance of social media. By not having a social media presence, you are giving out a message to your customers that you are not bothered. Your competitors who are active on social media channels will win over the customers who you are not giving a medium to approach your brand.

Ignoring Reviews

The user-generated content is a powerful influencer in making a purchase decision. If you ignore any negative comments or reviews about your brand, then they have the power of driving away your potential customers.

Bad Web Content

If your website has content with grammatical mistakes and overloaded with jargon, it will leave a wrong impression on the visitors. Low-quality content leads to an increase in the bounce rate, and people will lack trust in what you say about yourself.

Negative Press Release or Blogs

A negative press release from a renowned publication can do more harm than negative reviews. Let's say you are a travel planner, and someone who opted for your services wrote a blog about their worst travel experience. They expressed the negative experience they had with your services. You would like to avoid such a situation online.

Your Team's Rough Online Behavior

Sometimes your team can do more harm to your brand than good. Their negative behavior can harm your brand image online.

Online Reputation Management: A Step-by-Step Guide

Here is the list of activities you need to do for ORM.

Monitor Your Brand Reputation

The first step is to set up monitoring of your brand mentions online. You need to set up Google alerts that keep track of any newly published content that includes your brand name.

You can set up an alert for a certain keyword such as your brand name and decide the frequency of receiving notification through e-mail. You can also include the content sources that you want to monitor, such as news websites, blogs, or videos. You can set a preferred language and geographic location, as well.

Google Alerts is a free service that searches for a keyword mention in all the content that has been recently indexed by search engines.

Let us take an example. You run a restaurant with the name "Fiesta." You run a website and offer a mobile app for food delivery. You set up a Google Alert for your brand name, "Fiesta." One of your customers "Joe" who ordered recently from your restaurant was not happy with a delay in delivery on his birthday. He writes a negative review on Yelp about your restaurant with the title "Fiesta has good food, but its delivery is pathetic."

Now, as you have set up an alert, you receive notification about the review. Using Google Alerts is an example of how you can monitor your brand mentions.

Address the Negative Reviews

Now you know there is a negative review online about your brand. The next step would be to address the negative review. Your goal would be to turn the negative situation into a positive one.

Let's continue with the same example. You visit Yelp and get the details of Joe, who wrote negatively about your brand. You send an apology message to him and offer him a 20 percent discount. You also request the customer to remove their review.

This way, you will not only handle your online reputation but win a loyal customer by making them feel that you value their opinion.

So far, I have mostly talked about situations where there was something negative about a brand online and what to do to minimize the impact of any negative mentions of the brand, although a proactive approach would be to create a positive image of your brand through different channels.

Encourage Positive Reviews

You should not only address the negative reviews but should also aim to get positive reviews from the customers who love your brand. A customer with a positive experience will be likely to leave a positive review. A positive review will help you build your brand's credibility.

Let's consider the example of restaurant. If you have customers who visit your restaurant very often, you can ask them to write a positive review online and give them an incentive such as a free dessert or a discount coupon on their birthdays as a token of gratitude.

People will only submit positive reviews if it a hassle-free process. Some stores have the sales staff with tablets to prompt customers to give reviews on the spot. You can think of different ways to get positive reviews.

Highlight Your Positive Reviews

There is no better way to create a positive impact than having positive reviews on your website. You can ask permission from your customers to use their positive reviews on your website.

Get Positive PR

Another best source of a positive review better than user-generated content is getting positive reviews from a high-authority site. You can reach out to some PR sites and ask them to review your offerings. A positive review can outweigh any negative impression that has been created for your brand.

Use Social Media Accounts

Social media channels help to build trust among customers. Through your social media accounts, your users should be able to access you. The more available and transparent your brand is online, a better rapport you will build with your customers.

SEO for ORM

You can dedicate some of your SEO efforts toward ORM. Do some search for keywords related to your brand. These keywords can be to get reviews for your brand or your comparison with your competitors. It can be to find specific information about your brands such as your company's net worth, your team size, or any keywords related to the key members of your team. You can write blogs on these keywords and get these blogs published on some review sites or some marketplaces.

You can also publish these blogs on your website in the company category.

You can also dedicate your off-page efforts, such as getting backlinks from some high authority websites where your brand gets a positive mention.

Do Regular Surveys

The best way to prevent any negative response reaching online is to ask your customers what they think about your brand directly. You can send out surveys every quarter or every six months, depending on the nature of your business. These surveys will give your customers a medium to vent out their frustrations or any positive associations with your brand. With firsthand feedback, you can address the real challenges with your brand proactively.

Establish a Channel to Address Grievances

You should establish a proper channel to address grievances; it may be through e-mails, social media channels, or telephone, but you should provide your customers with a direct channel where they can raise their concerns anytime. This way, your customers will be talking to you rather than negatively talking about you.

In my personal experience, I have seen companies narrowing down ORM to positive reviews. A company with a lousy rapport in handling employees are prone to getting a lot of criticism on Glassdoor (company review site). The employees were going out of the company with a bad experience used to write in great lengths about the toxic culture and the absence of a sensitive human resource department.

The team responsible for ORM learned about the negative reviews on Glassdoor and how it is creating a negative perception in the minds of potential recruits. They decided to ask their team members to add positive reviews to counter any negative reviews. The idea was if there is one negative review on the site, the team will add five to six positive reviews. As only the most recent reviews are visible, any negative review will be hidden from the recent searches.

This may sound like a quick fix to the reputation problem. This strategy didn't work as it was doomed to fail. The ex-employees learned about these fake reviews and started adding more negative reviews mentioning about the false positive reviews. This led to a cobra effect, as the intended solution made the problem even worst.

First of all, it was not only an ORM problem, but it was something more serious. It was the problem with the work environment and the human resource practices in the company. Solving this underlying problem with just ORM will never give a permanent solution.

The crux of the story is that you have to understand that ORM doesn't address the underlying cause of a problem. You need to address the main challenges in your business practices, if any, to build a positive image.

Many people, who have a remote idea of ORM, usually think that ORM is all about getting positive reviews. They typically adopt the strategy of getting fake positive reviews. The problem with this approach is that it is easy to make out which review is fake and which is the real one as people are aware that not all reviews are genuine.

Second, by not addressing the real issue, you are leaving an open wound that will eventually bleed your reputation to death.

Social Media Monitoring

Social media networks are not only the best places to network with your friends and family. It is a great place for businesses to build a relationship with their target audiences. With social media, you are just a tweet away from your unhappy customer. You need to invest time in building your social accounts and keep a tab on what people are saying about your brand.

Social media monitoring is also known as social listening. This helps to examine what people are saying about something or someone. It also helps in sentiment analysis, which is data analysis to understand the sentiment of people about something.

In social media monitoring, you can track keywords, hashtags, or mentions. This helps businesses to become efficient and responsive to customer needs. Social media monitoring is a subset of ORM, which helps you manage your brand reputation on social media networks.

ORM Tools: Social Media Monitoring

Here is a list of free social media monitoring tools:

TwitterDeck

This tool offers a customized Twitter interface to monitor different search terms, users, hashtags, and lists. You can also track the content from specific Twitter groups. These groups may be the ones your competitors and/ or your employees own.

It is a great tool to monitor live conversions to keep a tab on your brand mentions.

Social Mention

Through Social Mention, you set a search term to aggregate all the images, microblogs, blogs, and video content from different social networks and search engines. You will get all this information in a single place. This helps to get a comprehensive view of what content is being generated about your brand.

Mentionmapp

This is another tool you can use to monitor the Twitter network. It connects you with a Twitter API that helps you find out who is talking about your brand and who retweets your posts. This helps you to analyze how a tweet can have a positive or negative impact on your brand.

Hootsuite

It not only gives you social media monitoring capabilities but also gives you analytics all in one place. The best part about Hootsuite is that it monitors all your social networks, not just one. This tool integrates with Twitter, Facebook, LinkedIn, and YouTube. It's a free service for individual accounts.

Followerwonk

This tool allows you to search the Twitter profiles and bios of the users who mention your brand. You can log in with your Twitter credentials.

Lithium

You can easily manage and respond to the users on social media using Lithium. The tool offers integration with Twitter, Instagram, and Facebook.

Boardreader

This tool is excellent for monitoring the comments section and discussion panel. You can get information on what people are commenting about your brand. The comments section is where people voice their opinions more freely as compared to social media networks.

SumAll

This tool provides you an insight into your interactions, engagements, and followers on different platforms such as Twitter, Facebook, LinkedIn, and Instagram.

Protect Your Brand Online

Your online reputation is not only threatened by customers' negative feedback. At times there are people who are deliberately trying to give your brand a bad reputation. These can be your competitors or someone you have rubbed in the wrong way.

URL Hijacking

This is also known as typosquatting, in which someone registers a website domain name very similar to your official website. For example, someone registers a domain name with Amazone to capture the traffic from Amazon.com.

As now users search for the brands through search engines, the chances of typosquatting have reduced as Google gives you suggestions with the right spelling for misspelled words. This problem still exists for relatively new companies that have not yet gained recognition among people and search engines.

If you search for your brand name and Google suggest you some other results, then you will have to wait for your SEO strategy to kick in.

To deal with typosquatting or URL hijacking, you can register all the possible mistyped variations of your brand name. You can redirect all these domains to your official website. Many tools give suggestions for domains similar to your brand name.

Social Media Squatting

This is the practice of creating fake accounts of a brand on social media networks. You might be well aware of various social accounts you come across on Facebook, Instagram, Twitter, and so on.

For a business, it is catastrophic that someone has created their fake accounts on social media. The social networks provide usernames on a first come, first-serve basis, and they are free of charge. It is somewhat easier for anyone to claim your company's username if you don't claim it.

The best possible solution for this is to create profiles on as many as possible relevant social networks for your brand name. For example, if you don't think you will use Snapchat for your business, then you may at least create a profile with your username as it may be useful in the future.

You should also create profiles with similar usernames as your brand. This will help you give you protected from any possible misuse of your brand name. You should also check that there are no fake social media accounts.

Phishing

In the phishing attacks, someone tries to get personal details from your customers, pretending that the communication is from your company. Phishing attacks are usually committed through e-mails wherein a hacker tries to steal the bank information of the customers.

These phishing attacks can cause tremendous harm to your brand reputation. E-commerce companies are more vulnerable to these kinds of attacks.

The best approach to counter phishing attacks is to communicate to the customers how they can identify your official e-mail address. You can send out an e-mail to the customers with essential points on how they can recognize that the e-mail is from your company.

Points to Remember

1. The Internet has given a voice to your customers to express their opinions. Not all of their opinions would be positive.
2. The user-generated content can make or break your brand's reputation online. Online reputation management (ORM) is the process of monitoring and addressing mentions of your brand over the Internet in a bid to build a positive online image.
3. The end goal of ORM is to create a positive public perception of an individual, organization, or entity over the Internet.
4. ORM helps to mitigate the effects of any negative perception.
5. The possible hits of a bad reputation online are:
   - Lost credibility and trust in your brand
   - Drop in the sales
   - Increase in the numbers of customers churning
   - Drop in the share prices
   - Discord in investor relationship and partnership breakdown
   - Increase in employee attrition
   - Your brand equity is harmed.
6. What could lead to a negative brand perception?
   - No social media presence

- Ignoring reviews
- Bad web content
- Negative press release or blogs
- Your team's rough online behavior

7. Here is the list of activities you need to do for ORM:
   - Monitor your brand reputation
   - Address the negative reviews
   - Encourage positive reviews
   - Highlight your positive reviews
   - Get positive PR
   - Use social media accounts
   - SEO for ORM
   - Do regular surveys
   - Establish a channel to address the grievance.

8. Protect your brand online against:
   - URL hijacking
   - Social media squatting
   - Phishing

Assignment

1. Set up a Google Alert for your brand name and set up a weekly frequency of receiving information.
2. Search for any negative mention for your brand online through search engines and social media monitoring tools.
3. Create a strategy on how would you address your negative reviews as well as how you will get positive reviews.

About the Author

Shishir Mishra is a digital marketer and an author with over eight years of experience in working with startups. He has obtained a marketing MBA degree from a reputed National Institute of Technology in India, and also holds a Bachelor of Engineering degree in Information Technology.

With a Professional Certification on Digital Marketing from Times Pro (an education initiative by The Times of India Group) and experience of working as a digital marketing consultant for startups across aviation, e-commerce, IT, and the telecom industry, he has emerged as an authoritative resource in the digital marketing industry.

As a part of his go-global strategy, he has helped startups from different geographical locations to build a digital presence globally. He is well versed in getting results for both business-to-business and business-to-customer startups through digital marketing.

He has extensively written for UK-based entrepreneurs to help them derive value from IT for their business. He has authored a blog site for Indian entrepreneurs that cover subjects like Technology, Marketing, Innovation, Finance, Leadership, and Strategy. In his writing, he provides crucial insights to entrepreneurs on the various dynamics of the business world.

Index

OTHER TITLES IN THE ENTREPRENEURSHIP AND SMALL BUSINESS MANAGEMENT COLLECTION

Scott Shane, Case Western University, Editors

- *How to Succeed as a Solo Consultant* by Stephen D. Field
- *Small Business Management* by Andreas Karaoulanis
- *Native American Entrepreneurs* by Ron P. Sheffield and Munoz J. Mark
- *The Entrepreneurial Adventure* by David James and Oliver James
- *On All Cylinders, Second Edition* by Ron Robinson
- *Cultivating an Entrepreneurial Mindset* by Tamiko L. Cuellar
- *From Vision to Decision* by Dana K. Dwyer
- *Get on Board* by Olga V. Mack
- *The Rainmaker* by Jacques Magliolo
- *Department of Startup* by Ivan Yong Wei Kit and Sam Lee

Announcing the Business Expert Press Digital Library

Concise e-books business students need for classroom and research

This book can also be purchased in an e-book collection by your library as

- a one-time purchase,
- that is owned forever,
- allows for simultaneous readers,
- has no restrictions on printing, and
- can be downloaded as PDFs from within the library community.

Our digital library collections are a great solution to beat the rising cost of textbooks. E-books can be loaded into their course management systems or onto students' e-book readers.
The **Business Expert Press** digital libraries are very affordable, with no obligation to buy in future years. For more information, please visit **www.businessexpertpress.com/librarians**. To set up a trial in the United States, please email **sales@businessexpertpress.com**.

www.ingramcontent.com/pod-product-compliance
Lightning Source LLC
Chambersburg PA
CBHW061321220326
41599CB00026B/4981